MYSTERY

ON THE

OTTER TAIL

A MYSTERY NOVEL

BY

THE AUTHOR OF

PIONEERS ON THE OTTERTAIL

ROBB FELDER

ROBB FELDER

Copyright ©2017 by Robb Felder
Published by Otter Falls Publishing
Cambridge, Minnesota 55008

This is a work of fiction; Names, characters, places and incidents in this book are products of the author's imagination, or used fictitiously, any resemblance to actual persons living or dead, business establishments, events, or locales is purely coincidental.

ISBN   978-1980336723

All Rights Reserved. No part of this book may be reproduced or transmitted in any form or by any means, electronic or mechanical, including photocopying, recording, or by any information storage and retrieval system without written permission from the author, except for the inclusion of brief quotations in a review.

MYSTERY ON THE OTTER TAIL

Now this once historic place just lies in a disgraceful state of destruction after the cheese company almost completely destroyed the Feiffer homestead to prevent anyone from discovering just how badly they were polluting the underground aquifer with their waste water.

Lying beneath the ruins of the ancient brewery there is a very dark secret, - - - -.

ROBB FELDER

MYSTERY ON THE OTTER TAIL

*To Barbara
who entered my world
and does beautiful things there.*

*To Kira and McKenna
two angels, who
came into our lives on a moon beam
and light up our evening sky
like two bright twinkling stars*

*For all of our beautiful children,
and our grand and great
beautiful grandchildren.*

*For Billy
Wherever You May Be
I Hope Your Life's Journey
has been A Pleasant One.*

ROBB FELDER

MYSTERY ON THE OTTER TAIL

PROLOGUE

It was the early 1920's. The Prohibition years were just beginning

On a warm spring evening in 1922, just after dark, August and his son Joe pulled the team of horses and wagon down into the woods behind the granary of their farm. There, along with the other Feiffer brothers, Franz, Hans and Lewis, they unloaded the load of equipment from the now shuttered brewery. This was the first load of the brewery equipment that they bought when prohibition shut down the old brewery in 1920. This first load contained a 300 gallon copper pot. Also on the load were two of the 300 gallon wooden fermenting tanks from the old brewery. They carefully maneuvered these pieces into position into the still open back end of the basement of the 'hog-kitchen' which they were building between the granary and the hog barn.

When these were properly positioned, they returned to the old shuttered brewery for another load. That load contained two of the 300 gallon wooden lager tanks. These also they positioned into the basement. The next load contained a wort filter and cooler and the beer kegging equipment and twenty of the 'half-barrel beer kegs, along with a bottle filler and about fifty cases of beer bottles. The last load contained a 500 gallon steel water tank and the steam boiler. These, they placed on the first floor of the hog kitchen. These pieces would serve the equipment below, in the basement.

In the next few days, they would seal up the back wall and add a 'steel-clad' door. There would be no windows in this secret basement chamber. The equipment would be concealed from detection from above, or, anywhere else around the building. The main access to this secret basement brew chamber would be through a secret 'steel-clad' door in the water well, which was located in the granary basement. The back door would open into a tunnel that would run down the hillside to the edge of the tamarack swamp.

When the basement was finished, they would complete the ground floor of the building with brick walls, windows and doors, a roof, and a large, tall brick chimney. Inside the main floor they would install the wood burning boiler for steam heat, and the large five hundred gallon water tank over a fire box, and a three hundred gallon mixing tank. These would also be used for creating the hog slop, which had many of the same ingredients as a beer mash.

THE GOLDEN YEARS

2025

The old Ford truck groaned and grumbled as it turned over and slowly came to life. Jerome Feiffer looked around the cluttered old shed to make sure he had enough clearance among the junk and antiques to back his old 2003 Ford - F150 pickup out of the shed. His old truck had been sitting in the shed for the last eight years; neglected, unused and almost forgotten among the rest of the old abandoned household items and ancient memorabilia. But the time had come, finally, to Jerry's dismay, but Barbara's relief. She had finally convinced him that it was time. It was time to move on to the next phase of their lives. They were selling their home and property and would be moving into a senior housing facility. Jerome was now 80 and Barbara was 72. They both finally realized that they could no longer keep up with the huge yard and garden, and large house that needed more and more repairs and maintenance every year.

As he backed the old Ford out onto the

driveway, Barbara came out of the house and over to the shed. The old shed was in the backyard behind the garage.

"Why don't you park the truck alongside the driveway, out front," she said, "That way we'll have room on the driveway to put up the tables for all our stuff for the yard sale."

"Ok," Jerry said, "Then I'll put up the 'For Sale' sign on the truck. Maybe we can sell it along with the rest of our antiques. But first I have to go down to the rental store and pick up several tables, and also get the 'for sale' sign and the 'yard sale' signs."

As Jerry left to run his errands, Barbara went into the old shed to begin sorting through some of the antiques and junk items. After working at that for a few minutes however, she threw up her arms and said to no one in particular, "I don't even know where to begin. I'll have to wait until Jerry gets back. We'll have to work on this together."

It was almost noon when Jerry got home with all the supplies for the yard sale. They unloaded, and set up the tables, then took a break for lunch before diving into the piles of antiques and junk in the old shed. They worked for the rest of the afternoon, sorting out the items and putting price tags on them and displaying them on the tables. Finally Barbara said,

"Well, that looks like all of it, except for the larger furniture items. We'll put those out in the morning. I also want to get some items from inside the house to put out.

MYSTERY ON THE OTTER TAIL

"Ok," Jerry said, "I'll cover the tables with some tarps for tonight. In the morning, I'll put up the yard sale signs around the neighborhood."

Barbara added, "In the morning we can also move the larger furniture items out. I've already gone through the drawers of that dresser and the desk, but you'll still have to go through that old steamer trunk that your aunt Rose gave you. That thing is still full of papers from the old farm and brewery where you grew up."

"I know," Jerry replied, "that old trunk has been in the family for well over a hundred years. I bet there's stuff in there from the 1800's and probably papers from around the 1920's Prohibition period. And also paperwork from the brewery rebuild in the 1940's and 1950's. That old steamer trunk more than likely came over on the ship from the 'old country' with August or Annie."

"Well, you'll have to get rid of it sooner or later," Barbara said.

"Yah, yah, I know," Jerry replied in a tone of voice that Barbara knew all too well as a lead-in to a statement of procrastination, which she knew he was famous for, "I'll get to it in the morning, it's getting to be supper time. Let's get something to eat

After supper, they sat for a while and discussed their yard sale which would commence in the morning. After a while, Jerry wanted to go into the living room to watch the evening news and their regular nightly programs. Barbara, the motivator of the pair had other plans, however.

"Come on Jerry," she said, "We've got to get the last of the stuff ready for the sale tomorrow. We won't have time in the morning. Why don't you watch just the news and then get to work cleaning out that old trunk, while I finish up getting some more household items ready. I heard there will be thunder storms moving in tonight. I'm sure glad you got our tables covered with those tarps. I hope the thunder storm will be over by morning."

"Oh, I think it should be," Jerry replied, "There are no warnings for severe storms on TV. While you finish gathering more household stuff, I'll go down to the basement and clean out all of my old home brewing equipment. I won't be brewed any more beer in our new place, and I've got enough to last for quite some time. I still have the mash kettle and the brew kettle, along with the wort chiller and beer pump, and an assortment of fermenters. I also still have all of my bottles that I haven't used in years, since I converted over to kegging my beer. The empty kegs can go also."

So, together they began carrying all the old brewing equipment up from the basement and placed it out on one of the tables under a tarp. Next they gathered more of the household items that they wouldn't be needing in their new place and filled out the last spot on one of the tables.

MYSTERY ON THE OTTER TAIL

THE MYSTERY TRUNK

After they had completed their tasks, Barbara headed for bed. Jerry however, decided to watch the ten o-clock news. He had barely started the news show when, of course, he dozed off. After about a two hour nap, he was awakened by the sound of thunder. He stood up abruptly, realizing that he had not completed his assigned task of cleaning out the old trunk. So, in order to not experience the wrath of Barbara in the morning, he stumbled out to the old shed. It was already starting to rain, and it was black dark outside and the lighting in the shed was minimal, with just one of the old incandescent lights, covered in dust struggling to give off its listed sixty watts of power. As Jerry opened up the ancient trunk, he discovered that he could barely read the old yellowed papers. He made his way back through the pouring rain and thunder and lightning, to the house. Barbara had gotten up from bed, awakened by the thunder.

"What's going on?" she asked, "What are you doing out running around in the pouring rain?"

"I'm still out there in the old shed, going through that blasted old trunk "he replied, "and I can't see a blamed thing out there anymore, even with all the lightning going on. Do you know where I can borrow a lamp I can use out there?"

"Why don't you borrow that desk lamp from your office," she replied, as she headed back up to bed.

So Jerry grabbed the office lamp, and got an extension cord from his workshop in the garage, because there was only one outlet in the shed. So back through the pouring rain he ran, to the old shed, with flashes of lightning lighting his way. He got the lamp set up and settled into the old recliner and started rummaging through the contents of the old trunk, as, outside, the thunder rumbled and crashed, and lightning lit up the night and caused the lamp and dusty old light bulb to flicker and temporarily go out. Jerry dug through the old yellowed papers between the flashes and flickers of the lightning. He pulled up a waste basket and began tossing a lot of the old papers that were meaningless and valueless. There were papers from the old Feiffer farm that were records of farm expenses, and purchases of equipment. There were records going back to the 1800's of purchases of horses and horse-drawn equipment. There were records of sales of livestock and sales records of the sale of barley grain sold to the old schuller brewery that was made into beer. There were even some old photos of the Feiffer family members doing all sorts of farm work.

As outside, the lightning flashed and the thunder rolled across the city, inside, Jerry dug deeper into the ancient camel-back trunk. He found family records of long-forgotten events from the lives of August and Annie and their fourteen children. There were war records of his father, Joe Feiffer, from World War 1. These papers seemed so important to him many years ago, and he shared copies of important records and photos with his siblings, Matthew, Henry, Mary and Mark. But now, as Jerry was nearing his own 'end-game', these papers now seemed just rather redundant. So he just tossed most of them into the waste basket. It was getting later and later into the night, and he just wanted to finish up and get back to the house and get to bed. He was getting quite sleepy as he was finally getting near the bottom of the trunk. He could barely keep his eyes open as outside, the lightning was still flashing and the thunder continued to rumble and roll across town. He continued however, processing the ancient paperwork.

Finally, he came to the last item. Oddly, he couldn't recall ever seeing the item before. It was a very old photo album, leather bound, and brittle with age. In it were some really ancient photos of the brewery, probably from around the late 1800's. They were mostly pictures of inside the brewery. There were pictures of his grandfather, August and Hans Schuller, standing in the brew house next to the shinny copper brew kettle. Other pictures were of other brewery workers that Jerry couldn't recognize. At the back of the album, sadly, were pictures of the brewery being dismantled when

Prohibition closed it forever. There were some pictures also, that were very puzzling. There was a picture of Hans Schuller, shaking hands with August Feiffer. In the picture there was also Jerry's dad, Joe Feiffer. They were standing in front of a load of brewery equipment that Jerry did not recognize. Obviously a sale of the equipment was being concluded between Hans Schuller and August. Even more mysterious was the last picture. That load of equipment was pictured in front of the farm buildings.

"What in the sam-hill was going on here. There's got to be more information here somewhere, about what was going on."

As he looked again into the old trunk, in the dim light, he didn't see any more objects, or paperwork. He was about to give up and chalk it up to yet another mystery of the old brewery. As he was closing the lid, Jerry noticed that one corner of the silk-like fabric that lined the inside of the lid was coming loose. As he bent over to try to look inside behind the fabric, more of the fabric started to come loose. When he looked inside, he noticed something was in there, hidden behind the silken fabric.

He reached inside and pulled it out. It was a very old folio of papers with an ancient leather cover, which was all faded and hardened by time. It had a closure strap with a brass snap, which was also time-worn and tarnished. He carefully picked up the ancient folio and placed it into his lap as he reclined the old chair and debated with himself if he should open it now, or wait until tomorrow. He was becoming very sleepy as he checked his watch and found that it was already well past midnight. He thought he would just rest his eyes for a minute before proceeding with this item from the trunk. As his eyes were closing, and outside the thunder was still rumbling in the distance, he found himself prying open the ancient folio, the old brass snap required a great effort to unsnap. Finally it gave a pop and he slowly pulled back the strap. It was so brittle with age that it almost cracked in half. He slowly opened the stiff dried out leather covering.

    Inside he found a bundle of very old and yellowed papers. Most of them appeared to be some kind of brewery records from around the 1920's Prohibition era, although some looked newer than that somehow. The first section of papers appeared to be legal papers that dealt with the closing of the brewery for Prohibition. Some were the bankruptcy papers from when Hans Schuller lost control of the brewery to the Otter Falls Holding Company. There was paperwork from when August Feiffer bought the brewery from the holding company after they had attempted to produce a non-alcoholic beer. There were production and sales records, as well as the recipe for the 'near-beer'. These papers were not surprising to Jerry. He had heard that story all to many times from his dad while growing up in the brewery. These 'brewery' stories were practically an everyday occurrence for the Feiffer family.

ROBB FELDER

They 'lived' the brewery because they lived in the brewery.

The next section of the papers, however were a shocking discovery for Jerry. He had never heard of the events and records that were contained in that section of the paperwork. Here, there were some kind of records of purchases by August and Joe Feiffer of a great number of equipment pieces from the old Schuller brewery. Jerry had recalled that the farm had purchased some of the water tanks and pumping equipment from the shuttered brewery to be used on the farm. But what Jerry was seeing from the old paperwork was a record of a lot more equipment than he had known or heard of. What was going on back then?

MYSTERY ON THE OTTER TAIL

THE ROARING TWENTIES

It was the early 1920's. The Prohibition years were just beginning.

On a warm spring evening in 1922, just after dark, August and his son Joe pulled the team of horses and wagon down into the woods behind the granary of their farm. There they unloaded the load of equipment from the now shuttered brewery. This was the first load that they bought from Hans Schuller and the Otter Falls Holding Company, which now owned all of the brewery equipment when prohibition shut it down. This first load contained a 300 gallon copper pot that had been the rice and corn cooker in the old Schuller brewery, and now would become the brew kettle. Also on the load were two of the smaller 300 gallon wooden fermenting tanks from the brewery. Carefully they maneuvered these pieces into position into the still open end of the basement of the 'hog-kitchen' which they were building between the granary and the hog barn. When these were properly positioned, they returned to the old shuttered brewery for another load of the equipment that they bought from Hans and the holding company. This load contained a 500 gallon steel water tank. Another load contained two of the 300 gallon wooden lager tanks. These also they positioned into the basement. The last load contained a wort filter and cooler and the beer kegging equipment and about twenty of the 'half-barrel beer kegs, along with, a bottle filler and about fifty cases of beer bottles.

In the next few days, they would pour a cement floor over the basement and seal up the back wall. In the back wall, they put a door. The equipment and the basement would be concealed from detection from above, or anywhere else around the building. Access to this basement brew chamber would be through a secret 'steel-clad' door in the well, which was in the granary basement. The well was covered with thick oak planks and a trap door. Another steel clad door, in the back, would open into a tunnel that would run down the hillside to the edge of the tamarack swamp. This was all covered over by dirt to conceal it. When the cement floor was dry, they would complete the ground floor of the building with brick walls, windows and doors, a roof, and a large, tall brick chimney. Inside the main floor they would install a wood burning boiler for steam heat, and the large five hundred gallon water tank above a fire box. These would also be used to heat the hog swill, which has many of the same ingredients as a beer mash.

THE MAP

As Jerry was reading through the records of this secret basement chamber, along with actual blueprints of the construction, his mouth dropped open in surprise and shock. He could not even imagine his dad and grandfather undertaking such a secret, devious plan. It was becoming pretty obvious what they were setting up to start doing.
He sat 'bolt-upright' in the old recliner and rubbed his eyes as the papers from the ancient folio went skittering, all over the floor. Jerry shook his head to force his sleepy brain lobes to awaken. Outside, the thunder storm had long since passed, and the three-quarter moon was hanging in a clear western sky. "Have I been asleep and dreaming?" he wondered out loud. As his half asleep brain struggled with consciousness, he slowly realized what must have happened. He got down on the floor and started gathering up the scattered ancient, yellowed papers and stuffed them back into the old leather folio. His puzzled, fuzzy brain was still struggling to process what happened; - or might not have happened.

"Did I dream all that stuff that I think I saw in

the old paperwork?" he questioned himself. He was about to start looking through the yellowed, disheveled pack of ancient papers again, but changed his mind when he looked at his watch and realized it was going on four A.M.

"Good God," he thought, "I've got to get to bed, we've got that yard sale starting in a few hours." He was about to close the snap in the folio when he spotted one more piece of paper that had drifted under the old recliner. He reached under to retrieve it. It was larger than the rest, and was folded over several times He debated if he should unfold it, or, just tuck it back into the folio and review all the papers later. Right now, his brain was still a little fuzzy, and he didn't know if he should trust it with more confusing, mysterious paperwork. But his natural curiosity took control and he wanted to unfold the paper for just a quick peek, before he gave up on the whole thing. He was actually, momentarily, thinking of tossing it all into the trash and just getting to bed. But that curiosity egged him on, and he unfolded the ancient paper for a look before deciding. As he began spreading it out on the floor, he immediately realized it was a map of some sort. He turned the ancient, yellowed map in several different directions to orient it so the writing was facing in the right direction. As he did so, he realized it was a complete layout of the Feiffer farm and brewery. Upon studying it closer it appeared to be more of a floor plan, but only of the basements of all the buildings. Closer examination revealed what appeared to be circles drawn into some of the rooms of only some of the buildings.

These circles all had some numbers and letters written in them.

"There's got to be a key for these circles somewhere," he thought, "but it's getting so late, I've got to get some sleep." So he folded up the map and stuffed it back in the folio, deciding he would keep the folio and map for now, until he could find a key for the mysterious circles on the map. He grabbed the folio, turned off the lights in the shed and headed back to the house. Barbara was still asleep, of course, so he tucked the folio into the bottom of his dresser drawer, got undressed, and crawled into bed. He could get only about two hours of sleep before they had to open up the yard sale. The eastern sky was already showing a faint sliver of light, right along the horizon, and the blackness of the night was being washed and faded into shades of a soft blue-grey color. It was promising to be a bright spring day. Just before he fell asleep, he decided not to tell Barbara about the map until he could try to figure out the map key.

As Barbara awoke, the sun was already a bright golden ball against a crystal blue sky, working hard to chase away the chilled dampness of last night's thunder storm, which had cleansed the air of all the pollen and pollutants. She smacked the life out of the blasting alarm and leaped out of bed. Barbara rubbed her eyes and looked down at her still sleeping husband. He had slept right through all three ringing's of the alarm, so she knew he was dead tired and had come to bed very late. She mercifully let him sleep a while longer while she went downstairs and opened all the curtains before making coffee. This was one of her 'endearing habits', as Jerry called it, was to open all curtains and blinds as a first action of the day and let the bright morning sunlight flood the house with its warmth. After the coffee was perking, she went back upstairs and got washed up and brushed up, then went into the bedroom and found Jerry still 'sawing-logs'. "I wonder what time he came to bed," she wondered as she decided to let him sleep in even longer. She quietly got dressed. She put on a light, bright blue pair of shorts and a bright pink, almost florescent pink top. She had read that sales people should always wear light, bright colors. Those colors will create happy endorphins to put customers in a relaxed, buying mood. After dressing, she went back downstairs where the coffee was just finishing up. Barbara was not a 'breakfast person', so she poured a cup and took it with her out to the yard sale. She set her cup down and began uncovering the tables, and folding up the tarps. She was just taking her first good swallow of her coffee when daughter Laura pulled up out front. She had the twins with her; Kira and McKenna. They were Barbara and Jerry's great granddaughters. They had afternoon kindergarten, so Laura babysat them in the morning, after her daughter Jenna and her husband Travis dropped them off on their way to work. She also brought some used clothing items from the twins for the sale. Laura would help out with the sale until noon, then daughter Brenda would come for the afternoon shift along with Brianna, Laura's other daughter and her two boys, Anthony and Mitchel. Jerry would, of course, be there all day, as well. Barbara and Laura finished putting price tags on the last of the items, as the twins played on the driveway with their usual toys that Barb and Jerry kept at their house for visits. Barb and Laura finished up tagging everything on the driveway tables.

Barb said "we'll still have to move those large furniture items from the back shed, up to the driveway and tag them."

They completed tagging the furniture items as Laura commented, "there is a real mess in the back shed around that old trunk."

"Yeah," Barb replied, "Jerry left a real mess there last night. I think he worked out there half the night, going through that old trunk. He'll have to clean that up. I'm going to have to wake him up now. He has to get the sale signs up, and then help us move those furniture pieces around to the front of the garage."

Jerry was up already, and showered and dressed. He had just moved the mysterious folio from his dresser drawer and put it into his bottom desk drawer in his office and locked it. He had just come downstairs and was putting on his shoes when all four gals came in.

"We're hungry Papa," Kira and McKenna said together, "Can you make us some breakfast. You make the best blueberry pancakes in the whole wide world."

"Ok," Jerry replied, "But first I have to put up the sale signs around the neighborhood."

"Can we come with," Kira asked.

"Can we ride in your old truck," McKenna asked.

"We love your old truck, Papa," the twins exclaimed together.

"Ok," Grandpa Jerry replied, "go ahead and get in. I'll get the signs from in the garage. Don't forget to buckle up."

They drove around and put up four of the signs on street corners leading to their street and saved the last one for the end of their driveway. The twins had fun helping their Great Grandpa, pound in the stakes with the 'really big hammer'. They returned to the house and Jerry made his 'world-famous' blueberry pancakes for everyone.

MYSTERY ON THE OTTER TAIL

THE MYSTERIOUS STRANGER

After they all had enough to eat, Barb said to Laura, "we better get out to our sale, people will be arriving soon."

Laura said to the twins, "You girls help Papa clean up. When you're done, you can come out and play."

After the clean-up, Jerry, Barb and Laura moved all the large furniture pieces from the old shed to the front of the garage, except for the old trunk. Jerry had to repair that torn corner of the lid liner where he had found the mysterious folio.

People stopped by their sale all morning long. By noon, they had sold almost half of their items. They had sold a lot of the household decorative items; pictures and other wall decor, several of Barb's quilted wall art, and a large number of Jerry's home-made clocks. Barb also sold several of her fabulous quilts and table runners. Jerry sold a lot of his tools and tool chests, along with a cedar chest that he made a lot of years ago, and almost all of his beer-making equipment.

Around noon, Laura and the twins, Kira and McKenna had to leave. A short time later, Brenda came by and Brianna brought her two boys;

Anthony and Mitchel. After the lunch hour, traffic slowed considerably. Barb said, "We might as well have our lunch now. We probably won't get a lot of people until after their work."

"That'll be good, actually," Jerry said. "Maybe I can get that old trunk repaired."

"Yeah," Barb responded, "I don't know how that cover liner could have become ripped like that."

Jerry played innocent and said, "Who knows what was put into, or removed from that old trunk over the years."

After lunch, Barb manned the yard sale tables while Jerry, Brenda and Brianna went out to the old shed. The two boys stayed with Great Grandma Barb and played in the front yard. The two girls began cleaning up some of the ancient papers that had missed the trash can and were scattered around on the floor. Brianna commented, as she noticed some of the dates on the old yellowed papers, "wow Grandpa, these papers are really old. Are you sure they're not valuable?"

"Nah," Jerry replied, "They're just ordinary old farm records. I've already pulled out any of them that may be of value."

Jerry brought a stapler with and was about to begin stapling the liner back into place when Brenda noticed it and said, "Wow, Dad," that tear looks big enough, like someone pulled something out from behind it."

As Jerry finished stapling up the liner, he

knew he was now caught in a trap. He had already said that he had taken out of the trunk, anything of value. How could he now explain the torn liner that Brenda just said looked like something had been behind it?

"Ok," he said, "looks like I have some explaining to do. But before I do, I want you girls sworn to secrecy.

"Ok," Brianna said, "I'll pinky-swear to secrecy. I love secrets."

"Ok," Brenda also agreed, "I don't actually like secrets, but this sounds like a fun and mysterious one. So what did you pull out from behind the liner?"

"Was it lots of money?" Brianna questioned.

"No, no," Jerry replied, "nothing like that, at least not yet. It has to do with this old photo album that I found in the bottom of the trunk. Look through it first, then I'll explain."

As the two girls looked through the ancient album, Jerry thought to himself, "I can't really tell them everything yet. First; I still don't know everything about all this. Second; I can't tell them, or Barb yet, about the map until I find out more about the key to those circles."

As they finished looking through the album, Brianna said, "I don't quite understand. These are just pictures of people at the old brewery, probably during the Prohibition time."

"Isn't that your dad in that one picture?" Brenda questioned.

"Yes it is," Jerry replied, "And that's his dad with him, your great, grandfather. They're concluding a sale of the brewing equipment after the brewery closed. The rest of that story is still somewhat of a mystery that I am still trying to unravel. That's all I can tell you for now."

"So what was the item behind the trunk lining," Brianna questioned?

"I just can't talk about that right now, until I get more facts about it. That's why I wanted a sworn secrecy pact, especially from your grandma. I just want to get more information first. Let's move the trunk over to the yard sale area, now that it's repaired. After that, we'll just take out the trash and take that old album into the house. Then we can close up this old shed for good."

By the time they got the trunk moved over to the garage, along with the trash can, and the shed cleaned up and locked up, it was late afternoon. They had a lot of traffic the rest of the day. Finally about dinner time, Barbara said, "Ok, I think we'll close it down. Let's get the few remaining items into the garage. Tomorrow we can get them listed on Craig's List and EBAY, to get the last of them cleared up."

They finished moving everything into the garage, and the tables folded up, Jerry would return them tomorrow.

"I think we can call our sale a pretty good success," Jerry remarked, "We got rid of about eighty percent of our stuff, except for my old truck and the old steamer trunk. Did anybody see anyone at all take an interest in the old trunk?'

"I saw a few people look at it just casually. One of them bought the old recliner instead," Brianna replied.

"I saw some grungy old guy with a rusty old brown Chevy pickup truck looking at it in detail," Brenda added, "he studied that tear in the lining in particular, asking how it happened. I told him it probably happened moving the chest around over the years. He asked me what had been stored in the chest. I told him that I had no idea, probably lots of things over the years. Then he just left without asking or saying anything more. He didn't seem too interested in actually buying it, and he never looked at anything else."

"That was really odd, mysterious behavior," Brianna added.

They ordered a large pizza for supper. After supper, Brianna left with her two boys, Anthony and Mitchel. Brenda also left to head back to Stillwater. Later that evening, after the six o'clock news and one TV show, both Barb and Jerry collapsed into bed early. It had been a very long day. They slept very soundly through the night. After breakfast they poured a second cup of coffee and began going over the results of yesterday's sale. Barb counted all the paper money, while Jerry counted the loose change and then they totaled it up.

"Looks like we netted about four hundred dollars," Barb exclaimed.

"Yah," Jerry said, "It could have been double that if we could have sold my old truck and that old antique trunk."

"Well," Barb replied, always the positive one, "I think we did very well. And we got rid of all that old stuff, so we don't have to deal with it when we move. So we have some extra moving money.

"I think we should take out a little fun money," Jerry said, always the frivolous one, "I think we could do a little spring shopping." Already he was formulating a plan in the back of his mind. He was thinking he should take a trip up to Otter Falls to see if he could figure out what that mysterious map was all about.

"Well, I could use a new pair of shorts and top for the summer," Barb said, "and maybe a new pair of shoes."

"Ok," Jerry replied, "How's this for a plan? You can go shopping, and maybe I can go on that fishing trip, that I've been wanting to go on for quite some time. Why don't you go up and get ready to go shopping and I'll run the money to the bank. I also have to get those tables returned and pull up the sale signs."

So while Barb went upstairs to get ready, Jerry went out to the garage to start loading the tables into the old truck. As he opened the garage door and daylight flooded the garage, he said to himself, "Where's the old trunk? I thought we brought it into the garage last night. Or maybe we put it back into the old shed out back. I better go and check. I just can't seem to remember."

He grabbed the shed key from the peg on the wall, near the back door of the house and went out to the old shed. He unlocked it and peered inside. It was totally empty; just as he had left it the day before.

"What the hell is going on here," He thought. As he locked the shed and made his way back to the garage, he noticed the knob on the back door of the garage was all bent off to the side, and the door jamb was all splintered where the catch plate had been, and it was lying on the floor.

"Holy crap," he exclaimed out loud, "we've been robbed.

His head was buzzing with shock and dismay. "What to do, what to do," Half his brain was screaming at him. "Keep calm, keep calm," the other half of his brain was telling him. Just think this thing through before you get all panicky."

The problem was that he had not yet discussed with Barbara, the mysterious map he had found in the trunk; because he just didn't have enough information about it yet. He was very sure that it was the reason that the garage was broken into, and the trunk was missing. Now he had no choice, he would have to let Barbara in on his secret.

As he was mulling this over in his mind, he got into his truck and backed it up to the garage. He decided he would get started on getting the tables returned. After he got them loaded, he sat down in a folding chair to contemplate his dilemma. The first question that would need answering was, why, and who would break in and steal the old trunk? Probably the guy who was examining the trunk so carefully at the sale yesterday would be the first suspect. Jerry had removed the folio and map, of course, but what if this guy thought it was still in the trunk behind the liner. But who was he, and how did he find out about the trunk and the map? What about the key to the map? Was it still in the trunk, behind the liner? If so, the key was no good without the map, and the map was no good without the key. Would this guy come back and break into the house looking for the map when he realized it wasn't in the trunk? He was still pondering his dilemma, when Barbara came out into the garage and found him sitting in the lawn chair with his head in his hands fretting about the problem.

"Are you okay?" she asked, startling him out of his dark fog.

"Oh, I'm fine," he lied, "I'm just taking a little break after loading the tables. I'm about to take off and get to the bank, and get the tables returned. You have fun shopping."

He was hoping she wouldn't see that the trunk was missing. He didn't want her to know about it yet. He wanted her to have an enjoyable time shopping without fretting about what he considered was mostly his problem to solve. So Barbara left, none the wiser. Jerry left a few minutes later, to do his errands. He returned home shortly to face his issues. He decided to call the police and report the break-in, but to avoid a lot of extra questioning and confusion, when they arrived, he told them that the trunk was quite valuable as an antique; and that was all he told them about it. He mentioned about the stranger with the rusty brown Chevy truck. They examined the broken door latch on the back garage door, and started to write up a report. They dusted the door knob and latch for finger prints and asked him if anyone at the sale had any more information about the pickup truck that this mystery person drove. So Jerry called Brenda to see if she would remember the truck and possibly a license number. Brenda was at work and couldn't take his call, so Jerry told the police that he would have to call her back after work. They gave him a copy of the report to file with his insurance company, and told him to call the station after he talked to Brenda.

Just as the police were backing out, Barbara pulled up.

"What in the world is going on," she asked.

"Well, it seems that our garage was broken into last night, and that old antique trunk is missing," he explained, as he coaxed her over to the back door and showed her the broken latch and door jamb.

"Oh my God," she exclaimed, "You don't suppose that creepy old guy that the girls were talking about last night, came back during the night. He must have thought the old trunk was an extremely valuable antique. I wonder how he knew that we even had one at the yard sale."

"Well," Jerry replied, secretly glad she had drawn her own conclusion about it being a valuable antique, instead of the real reason. He still didn't want to tell her yet, "You know, you can find out just about anything, or anybody, on the internet."

"I guess we'll just have to file an insurance claim for the loss, if it's so valuable," Barb stated, "By the way, I just stopped by to eat some lunch. I really didn't find what I was looking for in spring clothes here in town. I just texted Laura, she and I are going over to Riverdale Center after lunch and see what they have over there."

So they had their lunch. Jerry made a salad and Barb sliced the last of the hard-boiled Easter eggs on top. They enjoyed that with a glass of Jerry's great home-brewed beer. Before Barb left for the afternoon, she asked, "What are you going to do for the afternoon while I'm gone shopping?"

"I think I'll start going back through all the papers that were in the old trunk and try to figure out if I can, what made that old trunk so valuable. I still have all the stuff sitting in the trash can"

"Good plan," Barb replied, "maybe what that creep broke in for was really something in the trunk, instead of the trunk itself."

"Well, we'll have to see," Jerry replied, as Barb was leaving, "anyway, you gals have a fun time shopping," as he all but escorted her to the door. He didn't really want to get rid of her, yet he did. He just didn't want to talk to her about it anymore, until he could find out more about the map. She was getting way too close to the truth about everything. After she left, Jerry went to work. He took the trash can full of the old papers and spread them out on his garage work bench and began sorting through them again. Most of the old farm records he just tossed back into the trash. He didn't think they would help him decipher that map code. He went back up to his office and returned with the folio and map, and the old photo album. He unfolded the old map again on the workbench and began studying it. There were four of the mysterious circles scattered around the basements of the various buildings of the farm and brewery.

"Why four," Jerry wondered, "What did those numbers and letters mean in each of the circles?"

Some of the numbers appeared to be in sequence from one circle to the next. The circles all had a combination of seven numbers and letters each, and the same number of letters and numbers in each circle. Yet each circle was different, except that each circle had the same letter 'K', just in different positions. Jerry began working through different combinations of the seven characters in each of the four circles. He worked at the combinations for several hours, but the only conclusion he came to was that some of the numbers appeared to be dates of some sort, because the numbers were low enough to be dates from during prohibition.

Sometime after five o'clock, he called Brenda to ask if she recalled the mysterious strangers' license number. She said, she was not able to get the number.

She asked, "How are you doing, handling the break-in and the missing trunk? You be careful Dad, this guy could be dangerous."

"Yah, I know, "he replied, "I'm going to get a new latch for that back door and also a deadbolt lock."

Then he called the Police Department to report that no one had gotten a license plate number. They warned him to be careful and report any suspicious vehicles near his house. He went back to racking his brain trying to solve the mystery circles right up until it was time for Barb to come home. He hurriedly folded up the map and tucked it, and his notes back into the folio and took the folio and album back up to his office and locked them up, and got back downstairs just as he heard the garage door opener, opening the garage door.

Barbara drove in and came into the house asking, "Have you had any clue yet, what was so valuable in that trunk?'

"No," he admitted, "I haven't found anything yet." This was the truth this time.

"You know," Barb said, "That could have been on of your relatives from up in Otter Falls. With your dad's large Feiffer family, it could have been one of them."

"I know," Jerry said, "Last time I counted, I had about thirty cousins. That opens up a lot of potential suspects. I think most of those cousins probably still remember the old brewery and farm'

"Well you be careful, Honey," Barb replied, "and get a new and bigger lock for that back door."

Jerry went back out to the garage. He decided to set a trap for the intruder if he should return. He left the back door broken, just as he found it after the break-in. He also left the papers from the farm records scattered all over his work bench, but he took all the brewery papers into the house. He took a door bell button and placed it and wired it to the back door so that when the door was opened, the doorbell would sound inside the house.

After his little trap was set, he said to Barb, "Let's go get some dinner, it's a Friday night, so we eat out tonight. Did you have a fun shopping trip with Laura?"

"Oh, yes, we did," she replied, "and I found some really cute outfits for summer, and so did Laura. I'll show them to you later, after dinner."

When they got back from dinner, he and Barb watched the 6 o'clock news and several if their favorite TV shows. After that, they went upstairs and Barbara modeled her new spring outfits for Jerry and then they crashed into bed. It had been another busy day. Jerry was still frustrated with trying to figure out those coded map circles. He tossed and turned for a long time, mulling those codes over and over in his mind. Finally he slept lightly, but about two A.M., the door-bell woke him and he ran downstairs, just in time to hear a truck start up, out in front of the house. He got excited and mistakenly ran out the door into the front yard as someone in a rusty old brown Chevy pickup truck saw him and pointed a gun out of the truck window and fired a shot at Jerry. The shot barely missed him because the truck was already accelerating. He quickly ran to the edge of the street, behind some bushes, and was able to get the license plate number as he pulled out his cell phone and called 911. He gave the dispatcher his location and the license number and description of the truck that shot at him. In a few minutes, a squad car arrived. He explained what had just happened. The officer examined the front door area where he was standing when they shot at him. They found the bullet imbedded in the door frame and took it as evidence. As they wrote up a report, they told Jerry to get back in the house and lock all the doors and stay put, and call them if he saw that truck again. They said they had sent another squad car in pursuit of the truck.

    Jerry went back to bed, but he had a hard time getting to sleep. After sleeping only fitfully for about an hour, he got up. It was now about six A.M., so he went into his office and started working on solving the map circles mystery. He pulled out the ancient folio and map and began going over the papers in the folio. He looked again at the Prohibition era papers, still dumfounded by what appeared to be proof that his dad and grandfather were probably engaged in bootlegging during Prohibition, brewing illegal beer on the old Feiffer farm.

About seven A.M., he got a call from the county sheriff's department. The deputy said that a patrol car had spotted the suspect's truck on the north side of town and gave chase. They pursued the truck out of town, heading north on Highway 65. They pursued the vehicle all the way to the town of Moose Lake, but lost them north of there in the thickly forested lake country. The deputy went on to say that they couldn't follow up on it any further because it was out of their jurisdiction. They did however, put out a state-wide APB on the vehicle. He further stated that, "the vehicle plates were registered to a person named; William Buchanen of Otter Falls. You can file a formal complaint with the Otter Falls County Sheriff, and they will follow up pursuing these individuals who shot at you."

Jerry thanked the deputy and hung up. After he got off the phone, Jerry started thinking, "I can't tell Barb any of this. She will worry herself sick about it. And she will want me to drop solving this whole mystery map thing. I think I'll just let this thing die down and maybe I should just forget about this whole trunk - map thing. I think Billy Buchanen will not be back after being chased out of town by the police, but what in the world was his connection to the trunk and map?"

So Jerry put the map, folio and album back in his safe and got dressed and went out to the garage and cleaned up all the papers from the old trunk and tossed them back in the trash. When Barbara woke, they discussed the trunk issue briefly and both agreed to let the issue go.

Jerry was good with this; --- for about a week. But after many sleepless nights, he knew he could not let it go. Late one night, when he was awake at two A.M., he quietly went into the office and opened the safe again and removed the map and folio and album, and sat down at his desk and began again to search for a key to the mysterious circles on the map. He pulled all the papers out of the folio and spread out the map. He read through the Prohibition paperwork again. There must have been something he had missed. There were the records of August and his dad buying the brewing equipment from Hans Schuller and the holding company.

As he began looking at some of the papers that were in order sequentially, after the equipment purchase, he realized that these were production records of the bootleg beer that his dad and grandpa were brewing. It looked like they brewed about twenty barrels a week. There was a summary sheet by quarter, and another annual summary sheet. There was a set of four of these. When he compared the dates with the numbers in the circles on the map, a bright light went off in Jerry's head. "Some of the numbers in the circles corresponded to the annual production summary

MYSTERY ON THE OTTER TAIL

dates."

It was finally starting to come together for Jerry. He had, he believed, found at least part of the key to the numbers in the circles on the map. He was elated, because it meant that there wasn't a specific 'key' to the map circles. The secret was in the bootlegging records. So that meant, all Billy Buchanen got was an empty trunk.

Jerry looked again at the bootlegging papers. The quarterly summaries were rolled into a year-ending summary, and that date corresponded to one of the circles. The first year-end date appearing in one of the circles was 1923, followed by a number 30 and the letter 'K'. At first he didn't know what the '30' and the letter 'K' represented, until he read towards the bottom of each summary, under the heading; 'Sales'. There was a number with a dollar sign in front of it, followed by the letter 'K'. The letter 'K' stood for thousand, so in the first circle there was '192330K'. But in the circle for 1924, the numbers were scrambled to; '30K1924'. According to the summary sheets for 1925, they increased production and sales to; 58K, almost double the first two years. But for the last circle, production and sales jumped to 142K, so the circle for 1926 had eight characters, and was written as '19142K26'. So their income from bootlegging beer was $142,000. That was a lot of money, back in 1926.

But 1926 was the last year of the circles, and

of the production and sales records. So now a new mystery emerged; why did they suddenly stop brewing bootleg beer after 1926? They were making a fortune bootlegging beer. For the four years of bootlegging beer, they made about two hundred and sixty thousand dollars from their bootlegging operation. That was a lot of money in the 1920's. Of course there would have been overhead costs; people had to be paid to transport and sell the illegal booze. But Prohibition ended in 1933, so why did they end their operation in 1926? Did the ATF shut them down? Quite probably something like that happened. But there were no records in the folio or anywhere in the trunk to explain the abrupt shutdown of the bootlegging operation.

So, while Jerry had just solved one mystery, another one emerged. Jerry now knew that he had to make a trip up to Otter Falls, to the old Feiffer farm and brewery. He had to know what was under those map circles. Was there more information under the circles? Was there more information about who else was involved in the operation? He needed more information about the shutdown. Was some of the bootlegging money buried there? He knew he could never get an okay from Barbara to go back to Otter Falls after what happened with the old trunk. She would say it was much too dangerous. So he began devising a secret cover-up scheme.

THE FISHING TRIP

A fishing trip. He told Barbara he was planning a fishing trip. "I've had it on my bucket list for quite some time," he said; just about a month after the yard sale and trunk incident. Things had finally settled down quite nicely and neither of them had spoken about it since.

"Ok," Barb agreed, "I think you deserve a little get-away, after all that drama with that trunk thing several weeks ago. But you will need to take someone with you. At your age, you shouldn't be going out alone, you're almost 80, you know."

"Yah, yah," Jerry snapped back, "don't remind me. I'll see if one or two of the grandkids want to go. They will be out of school for the summer soon.

"I'll bet Zachary and Colby would love to go with," Barb said, "You guys haven't gone fishing together since we sold our lake cabin up on Lake Washburn about ten years ago."

So Jerry called their son David. "Heck yeah," David replied, "Fact is, I'd love to come along too. I haven't had any vacation time in about two years. I've been working like a dog, up on the Iron Range, repairing their taconite equipment, almost non-stop for the last two years. I really do need a get-away. I've got some camping equipment we could use and some fishing gear. I know Zachary and Colby would love to go, they've been bugging me to take them fishing. They'll be out of school next week. We going back up to Lake Washburn, where we used to have our cabin? There's that camp ground at the south end of the lake. We could set up camp there. How about a boat? We could rent a boat, or a couple of canoes."

"Ok," Jerry replied, "It sounds like we have a plan. I'll take care of getting a couple of canoes. There's a place here in town that rents them. I'll also get the food. You put in for your vacation. How about I call you back on the week-end and we'll finalize our plans."

Jerry clicked off his phone and turned to Barb. "There, it looks like we're all set. The boys and Dave are all going with. David wants to go back to Lake Washburn."

He was so glad that David had suggested Lake Washburn. Now, he didn't have to lie to Barb again, about his intentions to go back to Otter Falls. Now, all he had to do when he called David back on Sunday; would be to convince him to go along with the Otter Falls plan. Jerry called the sporting goods rental store and reserved two canoes for the next Sunday.

On Sunday, Jerry had another plan; sort of a 'plan within a plan'. Before he called David back, he called their former neighbor Ted, on Lake Washburn. "Hi Ted, how've you guys been.

Haven't talked to you in a while." he greeted.

"Hey Jerry," Ted replied, "We're all good, here. Good to hear from you, how've you and Barb been, and how's life in the city?

"It's all good Ted, all good. Say Ted, I.ve been thinking of bringing my grandsons up for a little fishing trip. How's the fishing been up there lately?"

"Well, it's been just so-so lately. You know we've got that milfoil again in the lake, and that cuts down on the fish spawn."

"Well thanks for the update, Ted, maybe we'll see how it is again next year, and maybe we'll be up there again this fall for deer hunting. We'll see you then, you guys have a great summer."

Jerry called David back from the garage, so Barb wouldn't over-hear the conservation. He asked David, "Were you able to get your vacation for next week?"

"Oh, yeah," David replied, "I'm all set, and so are Zach and Colby. They're really pumped, and so am I. We've got all our gear packed and ready to go. Have you got the canoes ready to go?'

"Not yet," Jerry said, "I'll pick them up in the morning. I'll get the food yet today though and pack the perishables in my ice chests. There's just one change to the plans that I wanted to discuss with you first. I'm thinking of going over to the Ottertail River instead of Lake Washburn. We've always had good luck fishing on the Ottertail."

"Well, that would be fun too. I haven't fished the Ottertail since I was a kid, and the boys have never been there. Also they could have great fun exploring the ancient ruins of the old Feiffer farm and brewery. But let me ask you, what made you change your mind and want to go there, instead of Lake Washburn?"

"Well, two reasons; first, I just got off the phone with Ted, our former neighbor from the lake and he says the fishing is just so-so this year because of the milfoil in the lake. The second reason, I can't really divulge over the phone Dave. You'll just have to trust me until tomorrow. I'll explain the whole thing on the way up there. All I can say for now, is that there has been some new developments regarding the old place, and I need you to swear secrecy about the change of plans for now. That means, don't mention it to Carla, or the boys, yet, or anyone else. I haven't told Barb yet either. We'll have to check some things out when we get up to Otter Falls. So, are you okay with the plans?"

"Sure," David said, "I'm up for a little intrigue. Zachary and Colby should have fun with it as well."

"Ok, great, then it's all set, I'll pick you up tomorrow at six, A.M. Remember, 'mums-the-word'."

After clicking off the phone, he went out to pick up the canoes, then to Cub Foods Grocery to get the food for the 'fishing' trip, along with several large bags of ice for the coolers. He came home and packed the coolers and his fishing gear, along with back packs, and all the rest of his gear. He was just loading in several of his shovels when Barb came out to the garage to see how he was doing with the packing for the fishing trip.

"How come you're loading all those shovels?" She inquired.

"Well," jerry replied, as he tried not to stammer with his answer/lie, "we'll need to trench around the tent in case it rains, and also dig a fire pit and a toilet hole, plus we'll have to bury the fish entrails." That was at least a partial truth.

"Well, you guys should have a good time, up there at the lake. Come in when you're done and have some dinner and get to bed early. You'll probably need an early start to get up to Lake Washburn for some early fishing."

Jerry ate his supper guiltily, and he and Barb went to bed early after watching the six o'clock news, and packing his duffle bag. Much later, when he knew Barb was asleep, he went into his office safe and got out the old folio and the photo album, and packed them in with his clothes in his duffle bag. But not before making several copies of the map and leaving the original in the safe.

He slept restlessly, and got up at five a.m. After kissing Barb good-by, she said. "You be careful up there at the lake, and drive carefully, I love you, and want all of you back safe and sound."

"I love you too and I'll try to be careful," he said as he left for David's house and got there by six, A.M. He of course, had the canoes and the food and his gear loaded in the old Ford truck. David, Zachary and Colby loaded their gear and piled into the truck. The first stop was McDonalds, of course. They headed north with egg mc muffins in hand. Jerry hurriedly ate his and began explaining why the change of plans. He told them the story of the ancient chest and what he had found inside. He told them the story about Prohibition and their great, great grandfather's involvement in the bootlegging business. He told them the part about the break in, and the stolen chest, and him getting shot at. He told his boys about the folio and the map, and the mysterious map circles, and how he solved the numbers puzzle in the circles. The boys all just sat there and didn't say a word.

Finally Jerry asked, "Did you guys hear everything I just told you? Do you have and questions? Are you still awake yet?"

Zachary spoke up first, "Is that a true story Grandpa, or did you just make it up?"

"Yeah," Colby echoed, "It sounds like a story out of some movie, or book, or something."

David spoke next and said, "If this is all true, or even partially true, we could be heading into a dangerous situation, with a maniac on the loose. Maybe we should have brought our guns with for self-defense."

"Yeah," Zachary said, "Then we could be like

on a secret military mission, like 'Seal-team-six' special OPS team. Like the one that the former President Trump sent into North Korea back in 2018, and took out their nuclear weapons program."

"No, no," Jerry argued, "We aren't on any kind of a mission. I just thought that along with fishing, we could do a little exploring of the old farm and brewery.

"I hope we don't have to do a lot of digging," Colby said, "I want to do mostly fishing. I don't want to spend a whole week digging tunnels, or whatever."

"Sounds like it wouldn't be just digging," Colby's big brother Zachary responded, "we'll be looking for buried treasure."

"Hold on guys, we don't know yet, if there's any kind of a treasure, or anything worthwhile. So don't let your imagination run away with you," David added, "although it looks like your grandpa's has run away with him."

"Oh hell," Jerry argued, in defense, "I didn't intend for this to become a big argument. I just wanted you guys to have a fun week on the river, fishing and camping, and with just a touch of mystery and intrigue involved. This is your vacation after all. I'm on vacation every day, for however many days I have left. So let's all just learn to relax and unwind and enjoy what the river has to offer. That's what the Feiffer pioneer family did for the one hundred years that they lived there, until it was torn away from us by a corrupt corporation who just abused the beauty of the river by polluting the life out of it."

Zachary then spoke for them, "We're sorry Grandpa, for arguing about our vacation trip on the Ottertail River. I'm sure we'll appreciate it more once we've been there. It's just that we've never been there, and you spent all of your growing up years there."

They drove on in silence for a while. When they came to the town of Brainerd, Jerry pulled into a truck stop for a 'potty-break'. The young Feiffer boys got some snacks and sodas, and Jerry and David got coffee and a donut. Jerry said to David, "you drive for the rest of the way. We're about half way there. I'm just bushed. I didn't sleep too well last night."

David replied, "I'm not surprised. with all the stuff you have on your mind."

They drove mostly in silence the rest of the way. The boys put their ear buds in and listened to music and ate munchies, or played cell phone games and ate munchies. Jerry dozed off for about an hour after they came to the town of Motley and turned north on the four lane. When they came to the exit for Otter Falls, David shook Jerry awake.

"Ok, where do we turn into the old place," David asked, "I haven't been here in about twenty five years." He pulled over near the Ottertail river bridge.

"Actually, there is no longer a driveway into the old farm and brewery. The cheese company had it torn out some time ago, after they almost completely demolished the entire farm and brewery. They did this to cover up their polluting of the underground water aquifer with the sodium polluted cheese plant sewage that they were dumping and spraying all over the old Feiffer farm."

"How did they get away with that," Zachary questioned, "isn't that like, illegal or something?"

"Well yes, - - and no," Jerry responded, "First you have to realize just how big and powerful the cheese company is. They are a multi trillion dollar entity. With that kind of power and money, there's an awful lot of corruption that they can buy and engage in. For instance, the level of toxins that they were permitted to spray on the farmland was at, let's say, about .001 parts per million of salt nitrates. But, the company lobbied and paid off the EPA to have that level bumped up every year as they increased their volume of cheese production. Instead of buying more land to spray the sewage water on, they just pressured the EPA to increase their limits. From time to time, they would get caught exceeding, even those ever increasing limits, and would get fined by the EPA. Over the years, they paid millions of dollars in fines. But for a company with trillions of dollars of net worth, they just looked at those fines as a cost of doing business. They have powerful lobbies in Washington and Minnesota, and in every state where they process food."

"Wow Grandpa, that's quite a rant against a corrupt corporation," Zachary said, "but aren't all corporations corrupt these days. And what does that have to do with why they destroyed the old brewery?"

"Well, I'll explain that later, as we actually explore the old brewery ruins." For now though, let's just drive slowly past the old place. David drove slowly along the old highway that ran parallel with the railroad tracks that led into Otter Falls. They could barely see over the tracks to where the old brewery once stood. The once proud brew house had stood for over a hundred years like a majestic sentinel, guarding the shores of the beautiful Ottertail River, with its beautifully crowned chimney and thickly eye-browed windows, like a castle on the Rhine River of Germany. Next to the three story brew house, like its little brother, stood the much shorter version of itself, the bottling plant, an almost exact replica of the big castle-like brew house. The two of them a matched set of beautiful golden brickwork that stood gleaming in the bright afternoon sun. It was this shorter golden brick bottling plant where Joe Feiffer built an apartment home for Leona and himself and the five Feiffer children, Matthew, Jerry, Henry, Mary and Mark.

Jerry went on to explain, "Connected to the beautiful brew house, flowing westward, was the mid-section of the brewing complex. This appurtenant structure was also adorned with a beautiful facade of the golden brickwork. This mid-section, housed the secondary and the final processing of that delicious golden beverage known as August's golden German lager. This part of the complex processed the barley grain into malt. In the cellars of this building, deep into the cool earth is where August's creation was aged to perfection, into a lager that would indeed make Milwaukee jealous. Finally the building at the far west end housed the malt kiln. It was a tall building, almost as tall as the brew house, but of a different colored brick facade. It had a high peaked and pointed roof, from which rose a tall chimney where the malt was dried and roasted for storage until it was brewed into the beer."

All that remained now, of this once magnificent structure was a disgraceful pile of rubble. The company had done a terrible job of leveling the brewery and farm buildings. As the four Feiffer's drove on further, they drove past the remnants of the Feiffer farm, the farmhouse, once home to August and Annie and their fourteen children, was almost totally destroyed by a fire. Also leveled in the destruction by the Lakes and Land Company, was the carriage and machine shop. Oddly, the granary was left standing, but the hog, slop-kitchen and the hog barn were leveled. The old barn was also standing, except that a wind storm had taken off most of the roofing, the silo however was crumbled into a pile of rubble. Most all of the buildings of the brewery and farm faced the railroad and highway. This was because at the time the brewery and farm were built in the 1800's, the main street of Otter Falls ran right in front of them.

"My God," David commented, "the last time that I was in Otter Falls, all of the buildings were still standing. But that was about thirty years ago. What a horrible mess of destruction by that Lakes and Land Company. It's almost like they had a vendetta against the Feiffer family. They turned the farmland into a polluted swamp."

"This makes no sense," Jerry added, "because we, the Feiffer family gave up our homestead so they could operate their cheese plant in Otter Falls. This is some show of appreciation. It's a real slap in the face to the whole Feiffer family."

"More like a punch in the gut," Colby added.

"Or a kick in the ass," Zachary added.

The four Feiffers drove further along the road into Otter Falls. As they passed what used to be the Feiffer farm fields, Jerry explained how the cheese factory disposed of the sewage water. by spraying it out onto the farm fields. He noticed the once active irrigators were no longer spraying waste water. In fact, they were sitting idle and rusted along the edge of the fields, along the railroad tracks, like they hadn't been used in years.

"I wonder why they don't have the irrigators working," David remarked, "don't they need them any longer?"

"I don't know," Jerry said, "Maybe they have discovered another method of disposing of, or filtering the pollutants out of their waste water.

MYSTERY ON THE OTTER TAIL

Maybe we can find out when we get into town. We can ask at the Otter Falls History Center. I've wanted to stop there anyway, and show you boys the diorama of the Feiffer farm and brewery that you helped me design, back in 2016."

When they got into Otter Falls, they went directly to the East Ottertail County Museum and History Center. David and the boys went to check out the diorama display. Jerry went up to the information counter and asked if there was still much interest in his diorama display.

"Well," the curator replied, "there hadn't been for a while, but recently someone had been in several times, asking about it, and about the old brewery. I didn't know him, but one of our volunteer gals did. She said she thought he might have been Billy Buchanen. He was an older guy, about your age, only really scruffy looking."

Jerry then asked about the cheese plant irrigators.

"Oh, the cheese plant shut down about four or five years ago "the curator stated, "they had polluted the soil to the maximum allowed by the EPA, and the pollution had reached the aquifer water. So they weren't allowed to continue to dispose of their waste water into the soil of the old Feiffer farm any more. So they had to shut down the plant here in Otter Falls. I guess they opened up a new plant in the town of Wadena."

"Oh, yeah, great," Jerry said, "Now some other unlucky farm family will get their homestead destroyed by this gigantic, trillion dollar polluter."

They're looking for a buyer for the plant," the curator continued, "I don't know what they'll do with the old Feiffer farmland. Virtually nothing will grow there for another hundred years, I guess."

Jerry didn't say that they were headed out there. He just said they were in town on a fishing trip.

"Well good luck," the curator said, "I hear they're biting pretty good out on White Pine Lake."

"Well, thanks, for all your information" Jerry said, as the rest of his troop came up, "well, what did you boys think about your diorama, now that it's on display in a museum?"

"Oh, it's way cool, Grandpa," Zachary said, "It's just like I remember it."

"I could hardly remember it at all," Colby said, "I was so little when we made it"

As they all left the museum, and got back into the truck, Jerry explained what he had learned inside.

"It sounds like The Lakes and Land Company has pulled out of Otter Falls. Their 'reign-of-terror' on the Feiffer farm and brewery is over. So we shouldn't have to worry about being harassed for setting up camp and fishing on the river."

"And doing a little exploring," David added.

"It will be a relief not to have them breathing down our necks all week. You know; the last time we were here was in 1985. Barb and I and you

MYSTERY ON THE OTTER TAIL

Dave, along with your aunt Mary and cousins Edward and Charles were fishing at the Springs. After you left with your cousins and aunt Mary, Barb and I were accosted by one of the Lakes and Land security guards, who pulled a gun on us and claimed he had permission to shoot trespassers. I tried to explain who we were and that we were just fishing on the river. He claimed that the river belonged to the Lakes and Land Company, and he would shoot us on sight if we came fishing there again."

He said "Shooting a Feiffer would be a pleasure."

"That was the last time that we were in Otter Falls. That was forty years ago."

Jerry didn't tell them the complete story, because he didn't want to scare them from enjoying their fishing trip. He didn't tell them that the security guard that accosted him and Barb was none other than, Billy Buchanen. The same one who had broken into their garage and stole the old trunk, and shot at him, and was now making inquires at the History Center about the brewery. "What in sam-hill was going on with this guy," Jerry wondered silently.

It was now about noon, so they decided to get some lunch at the Brew-Ales-and-Eats restaurant in Otter Falls. "One less meal to cook on the campfire," David said

After lunch, they drove over to the bait shop. where they all got fishing licenses and the bait; a couple dozen minnows, and several containers of night crawlers worms. From there, they drove out to the Ottertail River bridge. Jerry drove his truck down to the river's edge under the bridge, out of sight. Here, they unloaded the two canoes into the river and packed in all the camping and fishing gear and the food and coolers. They paddled upstream past the ruins of the ancient brewery on the river bank. They paddled further up the river for about a mile to the area everyone always referred to as 'The Springs' Here they found the big spring still bubbling up from the shallow prairie aquifer. They had planned to get their drinking water from the spring, but they found a sign posted at the big spring, warning that the spring water was no longer drinkable.

"Well it looks like the cheese company's toxic waste water has finally reached down to the aquifer, and poisoned it," Zachary remarked.

"Yeah, now we'll have to go back into town every few days to get bottled water," Colby added.

"Well, I guess Grandpa and I will take turns going in for water," Dave said.

"Ok, with that problem solved, let's get our camp set up so we can get back out on the river and do some fishing." They set up their tent, sleeping bags and cooking gear, after that they spent the rest of the afternoon, fishing up and down the river. By late afternoon, they had caught enough fish for supper, so they headed back to camp and proceeded to clean their catch. They had three nice sized Bass, two medium sized Northern

MYSTERY ON THE OTTER TAIL

Pike, and several large Sun Fish.

ROBB FELDER

MYSTERY ON THE OTTER TAIL

THE STOLEN MAP

Before dinner, Jerry brought out the map and spread it out on one of the camp tables. They all gathered around as he explained the map circles with the mysterious numbers. The boys just watched, wide eyed.

Finally Colby said, "So, there really is a treasure map, Grandpa."

"We don't know that yet," Zachary chided in, trying to sound like one of the adults, "we have to find those actual locations, in the old brewery and farm first."

"That's correct," Jerry said, "I think tomorrow we should begin our search for the location of those circles, and find out what they're all about."

At supper time, David fried up several of the fish and served them on a bed of wild rice, along with a vegetable. After they all enjoyed their supper catch, Jerry called Barbara on his cell to let her know they had arrived okay and had set up camp, and had already caught enough fish for supper. David called Carla and gave her a similar message. The boys also called their mom, Carla. Colby almost gave it away when he said that they caught a lot of fish on the river, but Zachary quickly corrected him by saying, "there's a river that runs out of the lake up here and has a lot of fish."

"Oops, thanks Zach, for your quick thinking. I almost blew our secret. Sorry, guys."

They started a campfire and sat around it relaxing and discussing the day's events. After a short time, they all crashed into their sleeping bags. They slept soundly after a long day of traveling and fishing. So soundly in fact that no one heard a sound, as the canoe slid softly up onto the shore. They didn't hear a sound as the mystery person, or persons rummaged around the campsite with soft whispers under a moonless black sky. They left as quietly and suddenly as they had arrived.

The Feiffers got up with the sun. The warm, bright morning sun shined into the tent doorway coaxing them into the outdoors. The boys wanted to do some early morning fishing. Jerry made for the coffee pot and filled it with the last of the water, and added coffee to the basket. He lit one of the burners on the camp stove and, and got coffee boiling in no time, saying, "Guess I'll have to make a water run today, I used the last of it for the coffee."

David headed to the table to start up a batch of pancakes and sausages. As he happened to glance over at the other table, he said to Jerry, "hey Dad, didn't you leave the map out on the table last night after we discussed it?"

"Sure did," Jerry replied from over at the

camp stove watching his coffee perking, "why?"

"Cause it's not there this morning," Dave said.

"Well, what the sam-hill could have happened to it," Jerry said, sounding very upset.

Dave began looking all around on the ground for possible raccoon tracks, saying, "those pesky little varmints will carry off everything."

But after several minutes of searching, neither he, nor Jerry could find any tracks. Just as David happened to glance back at the table top where the map had been the night before, he noticed some words, written across the top of the table. They were written in mud. Dave had to go around to the other side of the table to read them. "Hey Dad, look at this he shouted," in shock. Jerry came running around to the other side of the table and together they read the three word message, written in black mud. It said, "GET OUT NOW'.

Just then, Zachary shouted from the river's edge where he and Colby were checking their fishing gear for another day of fishing, "Hey Dad, Grandpa, down here, I've found something."

Jerry and David went running down to the river. Zachary pointed to a spot in the sand at the edge of the water about ten feet away from where their two canoes were tied up. "What is it?" Dave questioned.

"Another canoe was pulled in right there, last night," Zach replied, "You can see the keel mark in the sand."

"Well, son-of-a-gun," Jerry said, sounding very angry, "That son-of-a-gun has stolen our map."

"Who is this guy?" Dave asked, "Is he the same one who broke into your garage and stole that old trunk and shot at you?"

"I suppose it could be," Jerry answered, "I just can't be sure. I think I know what he's really after. He wants the map and the key to the circles. It sounds like he thinks there's something valuable in the ruins of the brewery. But without the key, the map is worthless. We've got to protect that key."

After a while, talking about the map and the brewery ruins, they finally decided to finish breakfast.

After they ate, Jerry said, "Why don't you guys go out fishing for the rest of the morning, and I'll just run into town and get some more bottled water. This afternoon we can do some exploring of the old brewery and farm ruins."

David and Zach and Colby got their fishing gear and bait ready to go. They got into one of the canoes. Jerry would be taking the other one. David agreed to fish from shore. They agreed that the boys would be safer out in the canoe. After they left, Dave quietly asked Jerry. "Are you sure I shouldn't come with you, Dad? You've got to go past the brewery ruins on your way back to the truck."

"No, I'll be fine, I'll go around the opposite side of the island," Jerry replied, "you need to stay here and keep your eyes on the boys. I know we didn't bring our guns this trip, so maybe I can find some sort of weapon in town for our self-defense."

So David left and hiked up past the big spring to the horseshoe bend, to the sweet spot for shore fishing on the Ottertail. After he left, Jerry went into the tent and dug in his duffle bag and got out the old folio and the extra copy of the map, and the photo album. He put them inside his shirt, as he got into his canoe and shoved off. In about twenty minutes paddling downstream, he came to where the brewery ruins were in sight. But he took the left fork around the back side of the island, out of site of the brewery ruins where he was quite sure Billy and his accomplice couldn't see him heading for his truck under the bridge. He was pretty sure they were already at the ruins, trying to figure out the map they had stolen, and he thought he saw them digging debris out of the old bottling plant ruins. But they would get nowhere without his key. He hurriedly paddled around the island and under the railroad bridge and pulled his canoe in under the highway bridge, where his truck was parked. He pulled the canoe out of the river and hid it up under the bridge abutment. He got into his truck and headed into Otter Falls. In town, he first went to the Otter Falls state bank. There he rented a large safe deposit box. He stashed the folio and album into it, but first he reviewed some of the paperwork supporting the map key. As he again thumbed through the papers, he noticed some writing on the back of the last page. It read; One is four and three is two. He read it over several times until he was sure he knew what it meant. He stashed all of the paperwork back in the safety deposit box, locked it and put the key on his keychain with his truck keys.

He stopped at the bait shop and got more minnow bait, two large blocks of ice and three large filet knives. He hurried back to the river bridge and again hid his truck and took down his canoe, loaded it, and paddled furiously around the island, where he saw Billy and his buddy still busy digging out debris from the old brewery bottling plant. He hurried on upstream to their camp. Everyone was still okay and the boys were back in camp. He unloaded the minnows and put the blocks of ice in the ice chests. As he added the ice, he noticed they had stored a pretty good number of fish in the chests.

"Looks like you guys did pretty good this morning," he commented.

THE FIRST EXPEDITION

"Oh yeah," Colby said, "Zach and I caught our limit of bass off that small cattail island just upstream from the horseshoe bend. And Dad caught two more bass from shore, along with two very nice Northern Pike."

"The one was probably a five pounder," Dave said, "but the other one had to be a ten pounder."

"Well, congratulations guys," Jerry said, "this calls for a celebration." He pulled out four beers from an ice chest and handed one to David and one to each of his grandsons.

Zach and Colby hesitated and Zach asked, "Are we old enough for these?"

Jerry replied, "In the civilized world, probably not, but out here in the wild, at my fish camp, I make the rules, and I say, when you fish like a man, then you drink a man's beverage.

They all popped open their beers and said, "cheers," and took a good first swallow.

"What do you think, boys," David asked.

"Boy, it tastes kinda fizzy," Colby said, "and burns the tongue at first. I guess I'm not too sure I like it that much."

"It is kinda fizzy," Zachary added, "And it

tickles your tongue all the way down your throat. I think I like it."

"Well, lets get some lunch," Jerry said, "And finish your beers with lunch."

They had ham and cheese sandwiches and some chips and washed it down with the beers. After lunch, they began packing for the expedition to the ancient brewery ruins, about a twenty minute hike from their camp. They each packed up a backpack with a bottle of water, a hatchet, a pair of gloves, a flashlight, a small miners pick and a shovel. Jerry also packed a small bottle of kerosene.

Zachary asked, "What's the kerosene for Grandpa, are you going to make a bomb?"

"No, no," he chuckled, "nothing like that. Back when the brewery and farm were operating, about the time of Prohibition, they didn't have electricity installed yet. I'm hoping to find some old kerosene lanterns that we can find for light."

When everyone was packed, he handed out the filet knives, and stated, "These are for self-defense only. Remember, they are extremely sharp and have an eight inch blade, which can be a useful weapon, however, against a gun, not so much."

They all put the knives on their belts, and Jerry finally said they were ready to go. They headed out, single file, along an old deer trail that ran along the river bank. They headed downstream towards the ruins of the ancient brewery. They walked along in silence, each one trying to imagine what lay ahead. Only Jerry knew what they were getting into, and it scared him half to death. The Feiffer troop followed the trail to a point where the river bank curved away from the river and curved around a half-moon shaped tamarack swamp. As they looked across the swamp they could see through the tamaracks; the ruins of the brewery on the opposite side. They hiked around the swamp and came back to the river and followed it further down to where the old bottling plant used to stand above the river bank. There was nothing left now except the basement walls that were still partially covered by what used to be the main floor of the bottling plant. They were still down on the trail, close to the river's edge and the brush obscured them from the view of anyone in the old ruins.

Jerry began to explain to the group about his connection to this building, speaking in a whisper, he said, "This bottling plant building was where we used to live when I grew up. That's why I know every inch of this building and the rest of the old brewery as well. That's why I don't need the map anymore. I know exactly where those circles are located. I'm speaking in a whisper because I don't know if those guys who stole the map last night might still be inside. I saw them earlier from my canoe as I was coming down the river."

They crept slowly up the river bank, using the brush to hide their approach from anyone inside. The front of the building used to face away from the river and the back door faced the river. Of course with the building completely leveled, there was no front or back door, just the shell of a basement with an opening in the back, facing the river. As the four Feiffer boys approached the back side of the crumbled building, they noticed that someone had been clearing away the rubble from the opening in the basement wall. They stopped and listened carefully.

Finally, David said, "I don't hear anything. I think whoever was working here is gone, at least for now. Maybe we can hurry and explore a while, before they get back. Let's go, it's already mid-afternoon and we don't want to be stumbling around in the dark." As they went down into the basement, they found that the main floor had been mostly crumbled away. All that remained was a small section of the floor above, in one corner where there was as small room. The door to the room was all rotted and hanging loosely by only one hinge. Someone had pried open the door. They carefully entered the room. In the middle was an old rotting, wooden beer vat. Someone had pried off the old rusted door of the beer vat.

Jerry explained in a whisper, "Back when the brewery was making beer; the beer was pumped over from the aging cellar next door and filled into this holding tank, which was packed in ice to keep it cold until it was pumped upstairs and filled into the bottles."

They all took turns peering into the ancient beer vat with their flashlights. "It's completely empty, and it doesn't smell like beer now," David whispered, just smells all musty and rotted."

"Is this where the treasure should have been?" questioned Colby in a whisper.

"I told you," scolded Zachary, "we don't know if there is a treasure."

"That's correct," agreed Jerry, "although the first circle on the map pointed to this room. I'm thinking; that whatever kind of a container there was in there, has been moved. We'll just have to do more exploring to find it."

They shined their flashlights around the small basement room. There was a lot of rubble, but no container of any kind.

"Well, let's try to find the old tunnel." Jerry whispered

"There's a tunnel?" Colby exclaimed out loud, "Wow, that's way cool."

"It should be over there in the wall that faces the main part of the brewery," Jerry explained, still whispering, "The beer pipe that carried the beer over here into the bottling plant ran through a small tunnel."

They shined their flashlights across that wall. There was a large pile of rubble in one corner.

Zachary whispered, "It looks like someone just piled up that rubble recently."

They began removing the rubble and discovered the opening of a small tunnel. The tunnel appeared to be only about three feet high, by three feet wide. After removing the pile of rubble, they began crawling into the tunnel, single file led by David. The ancient beer and water pipes ran along the ceiling of the tunnel. The tunnel appeared to be about fifty feet long,, but just as they were nearing the end, David exclaimed, "Oh damn, it looks like they also blocked this end with rubble."

So they had to remove the blockage, piece by piece and pass them back to one another, and toss them out into the room where they had started from. They worked feverishly, but it still took them about an hour to get the tunnel cleared. Finally they got the blockage cleared out, and they all entered another room. This room was quite a bit bigger than the first one. In the middle of the large room stood a quite large rusty steel vat, about six feet high and around, but open at the top.

Jerry proceeded to explain the whole set-up to the boys and David, "Long before this three story brew house was destroyed, this vat was used to catch the hot brew, or wort coming down from above, from the brew kettle. Inside this vat is a screen which filtered out the hops from the hot brew. This hot wort was not what was piped over to the bottling plant. This wort was pumped from this vat all the way up to the third floor of the brew house where it was then trickled down over cooling tubes and sent over to the fermenters, and then the lager cellar. When it was properly aged, it was pumped back through this room to the bottling plant."

"But where is the treasure that was supposed

to be in that other room?" Young Colby asked, still a believer in treasure.

"I think they may have dumped whatever container was in the other room, into this vat," David replied, "here, Colby, let me boost you up so you can look into the vat and see what's down there."

So he boosted Colby up and he shined his flashlight down into the vat. "I see something," Colby exclaimed, "It looks like an old wooden box of some sort, but I can't reach it. It looks like when they threw it into the vat, it broke through some of the old rusty screening mesh."

He climbed over the edge of the vat and lowered himself down onto the filter screen. He pulled the box up out of the hole in the mesh and lifted it up over the edge of the vat, and his Dad caught it on the other side.

ROBB FELDER

THE MONEY CHEST

FACE TO FACE WITH

THE EVIL DUO

"It's an old beer case," Jerry exclaimed, "makes sense, coming from the bottling plant."

"I'll bet that's the treasure box," young Colby exclaimed excitedly, "I knew it."

Before anyone else could speak, they heard voices coming through the tunnel from the other room.

"Shhh, be quiet," Jerry whispered, "It's them, coming back for this beer case. We'd better run for it."

"What about me," Colby whispered loudly from inside the vat.

"No time to get you out, just duck under the screening," Jerry said, "we'll get you out after they've left."

So Colby crawled through the hole that the beer case had made in the screening and curled up under it. He suddenly realized he had left his backpack outside the vat when his dad had boosted him up. He hoped his dad would remember to take it with when they ran, however, he still had the filet knife if he needed it.

Outside the vat, Jerry, David and Zachary prepared to run for it, as the voices got ever closer, now coming down the tunnel.

Jerry grabbed the old wooden beer case and whispered, "follow me."

They ran for another tunnel in the far wall where the beer pipes came through into the room from the cellars. They squeezed into the opening and had to pull their backpacks and the beer case through behind them. On the other side they dropped down about four feet into another cellar room. This room was also covered by the cement floor of the room that used to be above, but at the far end a door opened to daylight, or, actually, twilight. They ran for it and found themselves in yet another cellar room, without a ceiling. It was rapidly getting dark, but they spotted a crumbling section of basement wall and scrambled up out of the ruins, as they heard someone yelling at them to stop. It was difficult running and carrying the wooden beer case, so Jerry stopped and handed the case off to David.

They made a run for it, over the crest of the hill and down into the tamarack swamp, as shots rang out and they could hear the bullets zinging over their heads. They waded out into the swamp and took cover in the thick growth of the tamarack trees. It was black dark out now and they knew they would be safe there.

They all breathed a sigh of relief until

Zachary whispered, "What about my brother, is he going to be safe where we left him?'

"I hope so," David responded, "we'll go back for him after these guys leave and things settle down. They now know where the beer case is. So I think they'll wait till morning to either come after it, or start looking for the next one."

After Billy fired the shots after the Feiffers, he knew it would be futile to chase them into the swamp in the black dark. He headed back down into the brewery cellar. When he got back to the brew house cellar, his partner, Frank was still waiting there by the large beer vat.

"Lookie what I found," Frank said, and held up Colby's back pack.

"Looks like one got left behind," Billy responded, "and not just the back pack, I'd be willing to bet."

Billy's partner, Frank jumped up and grabbed the edge of the vat and pulled himself up, to look in. He shined his flashlight down into the vat.

"Ok," he yelled at Colby, "Com'on out from under there, I can see ya."

Colby sprang out from under the screening and lunged at the intruder and jabbed his knife into the hand that was holding the flashlight. Frank let out a scream from the pain and dropped his flashlight and fell back onto the floor writhing in pain and holding his bleeding hand. Billy jumped up and grabbed the edge of the vat and pulled himself up and pointed his gun down into the vat at

Colby

"Alright you little smart-ass, you drop that damn knife now, or you're a dead man. Now get yourself up out of there or I'll just shoot your young ass and be done with it."

Colby quickly climbed up out of the vat and jumped down. "Who are you and what do you want?" he demanded.

"I'll tell ya what we want," Billy retorted, "we want that damn box back, and it looks like we just got us a bargaining chip."

With that, he grabbed Colby by his shirt and ripped it off of him. "Here," he said to his bleeding partner, "wrap this around your hand."

Frank wrapped up his hand with Colby's shirt, and Billy said, "awright, now, let's get outta here," as he grabbed Colby, and thrust him towards the tunnel, "and anymore funny antics by you, and I'll just shoot your little punk ass."

With that, he pushed Colby ahead of him through the tunnel, with Frank coming along behind holding Colby's shirt in place around his wounded hand. They came out of the tunnel and out through the small room and out of the bottling plant basement, and made their way down along the river.

"Now, we'll just find the rest of them damn Feiffers and make us a deal," Billy said to his partner, "I suppose they're still hiding out in that swamp."

MYSTERY ON THE OTTER TAIL

* * * *

After Jerry, David and Zachary sat huddled in the tamaracks for about twenty minutes, Zachary finally said, "can we go back, to get Colby now, I'm really worried about him."

"Ok," Jerry said, "But be quiet and be alert, those guys could be anywhere."

They left the old beer case and waded back out of the swamp and went back down along the river shore to try and sneak back into the brewery basement. They moved along in silence and in the black darkness without their flashlights. They were just rounding a small bend in the river bank, when they ran right into Billy's group. They could barely see each other in the darkness.

Billy grabbed Colby by the neck, in a choke-hold and put his gun to Colby's head, as he said to his partner, "shine your flashlight on us." When the two of them were illuminated, he said with a snarl. "Ok you damn Feiffers, lookie what I found back there in the cellar, in that beer vat. Now here's the deal Feiffer, your boy here for that beer case full of money. Whadd'ya say, we got us a deal, or a dead boy?"

"Ok, a deal," David said immediately. "But we don't have the beer case with us."

"Oh, I figured as much," Billy snarled again, "so we'll just take us a little stroll back there to the swamp where you stashed it."

In the blackness of the moonless night,

nobody saw Zachary sneak around and behind Billy and his partner and Colby.

He carefully and quietly crept up behind Billy and drew his knife out of its sheath, and holding it in a stabbing position, he lunged at Billy from behind. He was aiming for Billy's right shoulder, to disable his right arm and hand with the gun in it. Zachary plunged the razor-sharp fillet knife deep into Billy's right shoulder. The eight inch razor-sharp blade severing muscle, and tendons, as it plunged almost to the hilt, almost all the way through Billy's shoulder. It also nicked the main nerve to his arm, causing his arm to jerk back and out to his right, away from Colby. As his arm flew up and away, so did the gun. It went flying out into the river as Billy completely lost control of his right arm. He howled in pain and dropped to the ground. Zachary and Colby both ran over to their dad and their grandpa. They all turned their flashlights on Billy, who was lying on the ground, moaning and writhing around in pain and grabbing at his right shoulder, as blood began gushing from the wound.

"Damn you little Feiffer brat, I'll get you for this," Billy cursed, as his partner ran over and took off his shirt to press on the wound to try and stop the bleeding. Frank helped Billy get back up and they stumbled off in the direction of the old brewery ruins.

After they had gone a short distance, Billy turned painfully and yelled back at Jerry and the boys, "This ain't over Feiffers. That's my box and my money, and I aim to get it back."

Jerry and the boys turned and began hurrying in the opposite direction, back around the swamp and up the river toward their camp. As they came to where they had gone into the swamp with the beer case, earlier, Jerry said, "We won't go in after the box tonight in the dark. We'll come back for it in the daylight."

Zachary worriedly said, "Are those guys going to be alright? I didn't kill that guy, did I?"

"No, no, I don't think so, that Billy is a tough son-of-a-gun," David replied, "but they both better get some medical attention real soon."

Just then, they heard a truck start up, over in the direction of the front of the brewery ruins.

"I'll bet that's them," Jerry said, "probably on their way to the ER in town. We shouldn't have to worry about them for a while."

They proceeded around the swamp and up the river to their camp at the Springs. They had a quick supper meal of prepared dinners. Jerry noticed that he had forgotten to get more bottled water when he was in town.

"Maybe I'll just drink from the polluted spring," He thought, "It can't be that bad. I drank from that spring all the time, growing up on the river."

After dinner, they built a big campfire and discussed the day's events.

Jerry said, "You boys really did a great job today, of defending yourselves. I honestly had no idea those guys would show up again. I thought they would be off searching for the next circle on the map. I really didn't think they would find that box so soon, and then move it into that other room. They must have thought we would also be pursuing the box."

"Well, I have never been so terrified in all my life," Colby said, "I really thought that Billy guy was going to shoot me. Zachary, you undoubtedly saved my life, thank you."

"Well, I'm still worried that I might have killed someone," Zachary said, "I sure hope he survives."

"Oh, I think he will survive, "David reassured him, "He appears to be a very tough dude, and I get the feeling we've not seen the last of him. Who is this Billy guy, anyway?" he asked Jerry.

"I don't really know him that well anymore," Jerry explained. "I went to school with him, so I knew of him, but we weren't friends. The Buchanen family used to live up the river, near White Pine Lake. But I have no idea where Billy lives now, or if he has a family of any kind. He just seems to be kind of a recluse. I also don't have a clue about that accomplice of his. I just don't know who he is. And I totally don't understand where he got his information about the possible money hidden in the old brewery. He said there is money in that old beer case, so that means that they must have opened it before hiding it in that old wort filter in the brew house."

"What's the plan for tomorrow," David

asked?

"I think that first we need to get that box out of the swamp, before our 'friends' get healed up and come looking for it. So, in the morning, you two guys, Zach and Colby can go fishing again, and you and I, Dave will go and retrieve our famous beer case. I'm really anxious to see what's inside.

After they had laid out their plans for Wednesday, they began making their evening phone calls.

Jerry went first, "We had a very interesting day today. The morning fishing was very fruitful. We have a lot of fish on our coolers already. But we didn't catch a thing all afternoon, so mostly, we just explored along the shore. I think tomorrow we'll try a different place to fish. We could be home on Thursday depending on our luck tomorrow.

"I'm glad you are all having fun and catching a lot of fish," Barbara replied, "I'll talk again tomorrow. Be careful, and I love you."

David called Carla to report on their day. "Fishing was great in the morning he reported. In the afternoon , no fish were caught, though, we just looked for some adventure exploring the shore line.

"Tomorrow," Zachary began, "we're going to fish further away from camp."

"Colby added, 'we've got a really lot of fish in our coolers already. Maybe tomorrow we'll fill it. Grandpa Jerry says we may be home on Thursday."

"I miss you guys," Carla said, "I'm glad you're catching lots of fish. Good-by, I love you guys."

"Ok," Jerry said after everyone talked to the 'home people', "Here's what I think we should do tonight. We should keep a large campfire burning all night long. I don't think anyone will be coming around, they're both probably in the ER for the night, getting sown up. But just in case, we'll be ready for them. Dave and I will keep watch by the fire all night, and keep it burning. You boys get some sleep."

"I'll take the first watch until midnight," David volunteered."

So Jerry and the boys hit the sack. At midnight, David went into the tent and woke his father.

"Nothing happening so far," He reported, "Just a couple of those pesky raccoons, somewhere down along the river, chattering away. Looks like we'll have enough firewood to last the night."

THE HAUNTED SPRING

So David went to bed and Jerry got dressed and went out and stoked the campfire and got himself comfortable. It looked at first, like there would be no activity on his watch either. It was a clear, but warm, dark starry night with just the sliver of a moon. About one, A.M. Jerry was already feeling very sleepy. He decided to walk over to the big spring and get a drink of water, thinking, "Maybe a cold drink will wake me up a bit." He took an empty water bottle and filled it from the spring and sat down on a large log next to the spring and took a big drink from the cold spring water.

He thought, "This spring water tastes okay. I don't know why the sign says that it is contaminated." He was wrong though, the cold water only made him feel more sleepy and groggy. After sitting there for a while, he gazed around in the faint moonlight. Everything began looking kind of fuzzy and milky colored. As he looked over to his left, by the river's horseshoe bend where there was another large log on the shore, he thought he saw the shadowy shape of someone sitting there on the log. As he stared at the shadowy figure for a while, it became more into focus. After a few more minutes, he saw the figure raise his hand and motion for him to come over to his log. Jerry found himself slowly get up from his log and hesitatingly walking over to join the shadowy figure. As he approached the shadowy person sitting on the log, the person came more into focus. Jerry began to realize that the person was an Indian. The Indian was dressed in the clothes of bygone years, that is, he wore clothes made of buckskin, trimmed with a lot of beadwork and with buckskin moccasins. He had long black hair and a band of buckskin around his head adorned with beads. The Indian commanded Jerry to sit beside him. When he sat down beside the Indian, the Indian spoke;

"I am the spirit of Billy White Wolf. I have come to give you a message; a warning, of things that were and things that are, and things that will come to be by your hand. You and I are blood. Your grandfather made a pact of love and friendship to my family long ago, and your father sealed it by blood."

"But, I don't understand," Jerry started to say.

"Silence!" commanded the Indian. "The spirit will speak, but will not be spoken to. Since the dawn of time, this land was given to us by the great spirit. We are all here for just a short time and must care for this land and not destroy it by greed and selfish behavior. Evil people have damaged our land, and have damaged my blood, but now you will have the chance to repair it. The gold that you seek must be used for this repair. You will take only what will be allowed by the spirit and the rest will remain in the bowels of the land. You are blood of my blood and my blood will not destroy you. If you make decisions based on love and not greed, you will be greatly pleasing to the great spirit, and will be greatly rewarded. When all has come to pass, you will realize the meaning of my message."

Suddenly Jerry realized that he was alone, sitting on the log. He slowly got up wondering if he had dozed off and dreamed all of the messages told him. He made his way back to the campfire and stoked up the fire again because he was feeling chilled to the bone even though it was a warm spring night. He sat there by the fire contemplating what he had just seen and heard but, he could make no sense of it.

"Was it real," he asked himself, "Or was it just a crazy dream."

By five o'clock, he couldn't stay awake any longer and dozed off. At six A.M., Zach and Colby got up.

"Hey, Grandpa, wake up," they said together as they came out of the tent, "we're starving, how about some breakfast?"

"Ok, ok," Jerry muttered sleepily, "go get your Dad up."

David got up and asked Jerry, "How did it go

last night?"

Jerry didn't dare trying to explain the vision that he had seen and heard, because he didn't fully understand it and he was sure that everyone else would think that he just had a crazy dream, He, himself wasn't so sure that it was nothing more than just that, a crazy dream. So, he tried to put it out of his mind and instead, said, - - -

"Everything seemed pretty quiet, except about four A.M., I thought I heard that old Chevy truck of Billy's, over towards the farm yard. But the sound didn't last very long, so I wonder if I was just hearing a truck over on the highway."

And so the day began. It was looking like it would be a hot, muggy one. The sun was already beating down through hazy thin clouds.

Jerry said, "It's the kind of day that usually builds up into very strong evening thunder storms."

So Jerry made his famous wild rice, blueberry pancakes again and Zach and Colby took turns manning the bacon on the grill, and they all ate furiously.

After breakfast was cleaned up, David said to Zach and Colby, "you guys can take the canoe and go up river a ways, and try fishing up there. Grandpa and I are going back down to the tamarack swamp and retrieve that beer case and see if there is any money in it, or, if Billy and his friend already cleaned it out."

So they all headed out on their separate missions, the two boys to fish and Jerry and David headed back down the river to the swamp. They found the beer case just where they had left it, well hidden among the tamaracks. They didn't see, or hear any activity over at the old ruins, or at the farmyard, however, on their way back, around the swamp, they thought they heard someone sloshing around on the other side of the tamaracks where they had just come out. They picked up their pace and practically ran all the way back to their camp.

When they got back to camp, Jerry and David pried open the box. There was indeed money in there, lots of money. It was all in bundles, wrapped in wax paper.

"Why wax paper?" David asked.

"Jerry replied, "You have to remember that there was no plastic yet in the 1920's."

They began counting it out. There were twelve bundles of five thousand dollars each.

"Wow," Dave said, "Bootlegging must have really been paying off for Grandpa Joe and Great Grandpa August."

At the bottom of the bundles of wax paper wrapped bills, Jerry found a small folded up piece of the wax paper. Inside he found a skeleton key. There was also a small piece of paper with the message on it that said 'four is one'. That was the same message that was on the back of those summary sheets in the old leather-bound folio that had been in the old trunk.

"What's that mean?" David asked, because he had not seen those messages yet.

"Remember, this beer case came from circle number four and I think it means that this key is to unlock something at circle number one."

Along with all the loot, Jerry found some paperwork. There were journals of what appeared to be sales of the bootlegged beer. The journals were dated 1926. Each one had a name at the top. There were three journals for each person. These must have been quarterly sales reports, Jerry thought. He didn't have time to look through all of them. There were a lot of them, probably ten or fifteen journals.

"Looks like Grandpa had a pretty good sized sales staff for his bootlegging business," Jerry said.

"Yah, it looks like they had a pretty good sized operation," Jerry said, "and profitable too. Well, I don't know yet if all this paper money is actually worth anything. I'm going to run this into the bank in town and have them check over the bills to see if they are still good. Some of these bills may be out of circulation. In which case, they are worthless. The bills are all dated from the 1920's. That's about one hundred years old. Well, I'd better get going into town with these before we get company from whom ever we heard sloshing around in the swamp, earlier."

As he was packing up the money and paperwork into his duffle bag, he happened to notice one of the sales journals had the name Buchanen at the top of it and it made him wonder, "hmm - - -, that name, I wonder what the story is there."

MYSTERY ON THE OTTER TAIL

He zipped up the bag and put it into his canoe, as he said to Dave, "I've got to get this out of our camp, in case Billy and his Buddy show up again. I'll see you in about an hour or two."

He paddled rapidly down the river under ever thickening skies. When he came to the river bend where he could see the brewery ruins, he didn't see any activity of any kind, but he went around the far side of the island like before. He got to the highway bridge and stashed his canoe, loaded the duffle into his truck and took off for Otter Falls. He went directly to the Otter Falls State Bank and asked to talk to the head teller. He explained what he had in the duffle bag. The teller took him to a private office where they spread out the bundles of the bills on the desk. The teller asked him, "Where did you get all of this old money?"

Jerry replied, "We found it in an old building on the farm."

That was the truth, in a way, at least not a complete lie. The teller didn't know him and of course not his connection to the old brewery. After looking through several of the bundles of the bills, the teller said, "It looks like these are from around 1926 and earlier. The smaller bills, the 'ones, twos, fives, tens and twenty' dollar bills have all gone out of circulation. The Federal Reserve re-issues the lower denominations more frequently because they are used more. Those are pretty worthless. These larger ones here though, the fifty's and one hundreds are all still good."

"Ok," Jerry said, "Let's separate those out and count them, then I want to open an account and deposit them."

So while the head teller went to get the necessary paperwork for him to open the account, Jerry separated out all the smaller bills. After he filled out the paperwork to open an account, they both began counting the good bills and ran them through an automatic bill counter.

"Looks like you've got forty five thousand, six hundred and fifty dollars," the teller said.

"Good," Jerry said, "I want to deposit it all into my new account."

As teller completed the transaction, Jerry wrapped the old, 'out-of-circulation' bills into the wax paper again and put the bundles back into his duffle bag. He had a vague idea what he was going to do with them. He took his receipt from the teller and they shook hands and Jerry thanked him for his help. He left the teller's office and went downstairs to his safe deposit box. Here he put all the sales journals into his safe deposit box where he had the other old papers.

But before he left Otter Falls, he carefully drove over to the hospital. He parked in the back of the lot and waited. Before too long, he saw that rusty old brown Chevy truck pull into the lot and pull up to the main door where patients are picked up. A few minutes later Frank came out with Billy, who looked very pale and still in a lot of pain. Just as he suspected, Billy had spent the night in the hospital and his partner was now picking him up. Jerry carefully and quietly exited the back of the lot and high-tailed it for the river. As he drove, he thought, "So that's who I heard last night and again this morning in the swamp. It was Billy's partner. And that's why no one showed up at our camp yet. With Billy still in the hospital, his partner didn't dare risk it alone. It would have been four against one, and without a gun, he could have ended up like Billy, or even worse, with our 'knife-wielding ninjas'."

So Jerry figured; that being the case for hesitation on their part, now would be a good time for the Feiffers to do a little more exploring. He got to the bridge and launched the canoe and threw in the duffle bag and rushed back to camp under increasingly heavy looking and darkening skies. When he got back to their camp, the boys were all back from fishing and were having lunch.

"How'd you guys do this morning," he asked?

"Wow," Colby answered, "this was the best day ever."

"We caught so many fish today," Zach added, "we paddled all the way up to White Pine Lake and fished just below the dam."

"We caught our limit of bass," Colby chimed in excitedly.

"And we were pulling in sunnys, one after another," Zach finished saying, "we probably caught twenty of them, I think that's a limit of those too."

"And," David added, "You'll also be proud to know, they already cleaned them and stored them in the coolers and buried the entrails. And, I also had great luck, right here at the horseshoe bend. The walleyes were finally hitting, and I caught three very nice sized ones."

"Wow," Jerry exclaimed, "That's a super, good job guys. I brought back some more ice to cover the new fish. I'm going to grab some lunch while you guys pack up for another expedition to the old ruins."

Before there were any objections, he explained to them what he had done with the money and what he had learned about their nemesis, Billy and his partner. Jerry took the worthless money out of his duffle bag, and put the wax paper wrapped bundles of bills back into the old beer case, and put it inside the tent, in a corner and covered it. His thinking was that if Billy, or partner had to really look for it, they would be more likely to believe the money was valuable. By the time they found out it was worthless, the Feiffers would have returned to the city.

Before they all finished packing their packs again, Jerry said, "Pack some extra food for supper, in case we have to spend the night in the ruins. There's a real bad storm brewing, and we may have to spend the night in the granary or barn."

"Oh, oh," David said, Look's like we're out of the bottled water."

"Ok, each of you, just take an empty bottle

and fill it from the spring," Jerry said, "It should be okay just this once. I had a drink from the spring last night and I'm still alive today. It actually doesn't taste too bad."

He had already completely forgotten his haunting visit/dream from Billy White Wolf from last night.

Jerry explained that they were heading to the old farmyard, specifically, the old granary, which was one of the only buildings still standing, after the destruction by The Lakes and Land Company. "From there," he said, "maybe we can get down into the hog kitchen basement, where the bootlegging took place."

ROBB FELDER

MYSTERY ON THE OTTER TAIL

1923

The winter winds of January were bringing with them a swirling whiteout of heavy snow and below zero temperatures. Inside the basement of the hog kitchen however, it was toasty warm. The Feiffer miniature brew house was being fired up for the first time. On the main floor, the furnace was being stoked with some real heat-producing oak logs. Another fire was blazing under the water tank. The hog swill mixing tank had been filled with four hundred pounds of the finest Feiffer-produced barley malt and two hundred gallons of water, heated to one hundred, fifty degrees, along with fifty pounds of a pre-cooked corn mash. The mixture sat for a rest period of one hour at that temperature and was then heated up to one hundred seventy degrees. It was now ready to be sparged with a hundred gallons of one hundred seventy degree water. Franz had been stoking the fires and monitoring the water temperature. When the water reached one hundred seventy degrees, Franz hurried down to the granary basement and through the trapdoor in the well, and into the basement brew house.

"The waters ready," he announced to his dad, August.

"Ok," August said, "Here goes our first batch of beer."

He opened the valve and began draining the mash tank which had a screen mesh near the bottom to filter out the spent grains. At the same time he opened up the valve to allow the heated water to spray into the mash tank, over the top of the mash. As the sparged wort drained into the brew kettle, August took a sample into a hydrometer flask and checked it.

"Perfect," he declared as he read the hydrometer, "Right at 1.050. Open up the steam valve and let the steam into the heating coil in the brew kettle."

Joe opened the steam valve as the wort finished draining into the brew kettle. When the wort reached the boiling point, the first addition of German hops was added to the brew. The brew would boil for one hour, with another addition of hops at the last ten minutes. While the batch was cooking, August got his sons together for a meeting. There was Joe, Franz, Hans and Lewis.

"Well boys, it looks like our little basement brewery is working pretty darn well. Now we've got to go over the plans for selling our great German lager. This first batch, when it's done brewing, will go into the fermenter for two weeks, then into the lager tank for a month. We'll brew one batch a week. That's twelve hundred of the thirty two ounce bottles, or a hundred, fifty cases per week, or twenty half-barrel kegs."

"Lewis, you're in charge of selling, and you said you have several speak-easies lined up, ready to start taking shipments in a month and a half. We'll keep everything top secret, so nobody, except you and I will know where we're selling the beer. You will coordinate with the delivery drivers, whose names will be kept secret. They will pick up two loads of seventy five cases, or ten of the half barrel kegs a week from our warehouse, hidden in a load of milled feed. The location will remain secret. Only Hans and the other drivers will know where it is and Hans will make two runs a week from here to the warehouse. The beer will be hidden in a load of sacks of grain being delivered to the warehouse, which will be an actual feed mill."

"Lewis will collect the sales money and put it into a safe deposit box in the First National Bank of Moorhead. Hans will pick up the money twice a month and bring it back here where he will reconcile the records with the quantity that we are brewing. I will take care of it once the books are balanced. No one will know where it goes except me. Franz is in charge of keeping up the wood supply and stoking the fires in the boiler and the hot water tank and monitoring the temperatures.

He will also be getting the barley grain spread out on the granary basement floor for malting. Joe will complete the malting and the roasting in the malt kiln. He will also do the mashing and he will be in charge of brewing when I'm not available."

"Remember, everything is top secret. Nobody knows what anybody else does. The rest of our family is not to know about any of this operation, ever. Not even your mother."

"In between brewing and delivering and selling, we still have to run the farm. So everyone will keep doing their regular jobs on the farm, when not brewing. In the event that we should be visited by the ATF boys, just stay calm and go to performing your regular farming jobs. If we have a beer mash going when they visit, be ready to mix in a bunch of ground oats and corn to dilute it down and immediately feed it to the hogs. And remember to always keep the steel doors locked at all times, and the trapdoor closed."

MYSTERY ON THE OTTER TAIL

THE HAUNTED CHAMBER

The young Feiffers headed out in a hurry as a very black cloud was looming across the western side of the prairie. By the time they reached the old granary, it was beginning to thunder and lightning. As they approached the old farm buildings, they noticed the old barn was leaning from a previous wind storm, the roof, missing shingles, the same for the hog barn. The old silo was only partially standing. The old cement blocks were crumbling and caving in. The ancient hog kitchen, where the hog slop was at one time mixed was almost completely leveled. All that was left of the old brick building were a few piles of brick debris with weeds and brush growing out of them. But the old concrete floor was intact, beneath the rubble. They hurried across the floor and quickly went inside the granary's first floor. As they entered, they heard noises that were not from the thunder outside. They immediately fell into silence.

Jerry had his suspicions, so he went to a front window and peered out. The storm had turned it black dark outside, but as the lightning clashed, he could make out a large object right out front. And as a flash real close by completely illuminated it, he could now make out, the old rusty brown Chevy truck. He turned back to the others, "We've got to get out of here," he whispered. He led them back out into the pouring rain. The lightning flashed and the thunder rolled across the prairie as Jerry led them around back and down to a basement door. The door was unlocked, so they all hurriedly went inside. They shook the water off of themselves as Jerry explained, "We'll be safe in here for now. They won't hear us up on the third floor. The floor above us is built very thick and is pretty sound proof, and there is no stairway going up from here. The only entrance is from that outside door, where we just came in."

"So what's going on?" Questioned Dave, and what did you see out front."

"They're here," Jerry declared, almost shouting, with a great deal of fear and panic in his voice, "I saw his old rusty brown truck outside."

"What the hell would they be doing here, in this thunderstorm?" David questioned again.

"Well, that Billy is such a damn recluse. It wouldn't surprise me, if he's actually living here, in this granary. Maybe up on the third floor. This building is one of the only ones left standing after that cheese company destroyed everything else."

"So, what do we do now?" Colby asked?

"Do we stand and fight them again?" Zachary asked, "or, do we just run for it?'

"I don't think we should fight them again," David answered his boys, "we got lucky that first time. They might have retrieved their gun from the river, or, they may have more of them upstairs. Who knows?"

"Ok, Dad, but what about the fact that they are pretty wounded after last night," Colby argued.

"Still," David replied, "in a fight with guns against knives, guns will win ninety nine percent of the time. I just don't like those odds."

"Ok, ok, hold on," Jerry retorted, "maybe we don't have to do either one, fight, or run. Maybe we should just stick to the original plan, which was, to look for circle number one under the hog kitchen. If we can find the entrance to it, we should be even safer inside there."

Outside, the lightning was flashing as the thunder storm rolled across the prairie and slammed into the ancient granary, and the thunder reverberated and shook the building, as it echoed out across the river valley. Inside the granary, the Feiffers shined their flashlights around the granary basement. There was the large grain bin in the middle of the front wall, where the grain was unloaded above, outside, and came down a chute into the bin where it was shoveled into the mouth of the elevator. Outside the bin and elevator there still sat the old giant gasoline engine that had motorized the elevator. The basement was strewn with old elevator parts and grain tubing, and other miscellaneous parts. They shined their lights and carefully stepped over these parts, being careful not to bang into the large metal grain chutes. That noise would carry right up the ancient elevator shaft to the third floor. They slowly and quietly followed Jerry around the grain bin to a corner area of the basement where the ancient well was located. The well pipe had long ago been pulled up and removed, as had all well pipes on the farm and houses and the brewery. This was so that no one would pull up the polluted water from the aquifer that the cheese company was poisoning.

Jerry recalled that the well shaft itself was about four feet square and was about twenty feet deep. They shined their flashlights over there and found that the well was sealed with a thick plank covering, with a two inch hole drilled into the center where the old well pipe had been. Jerry got down on his hands and knees and brushed a thick layer of dust off of the covering. There appeared to be a trap door in the plank covering and it was fitted tightly into the frame. There was no metal handle or ring to pull it open, (like you see in movies). They would need a large sharp object to try and pry it open. David and the boys scoured around the basement until they found a steel bar with a pointed end.

Jerry took the bar and jabbed at the edge of the trapdoor. He tried to be careful to try and do it quietly because of their upstairs neighbors. As the lightning flashed outside and the thunder rolled across the prairie and shook the granary, Jerry tried to time his hits on the trapdoor to coincide with the thunder. After about a dozen or so jabs, he finally had chipped a hole in the edge of the thick planked trapdoor, large enough to stick the steel bar into and begin prying.

It took both Jerry and David together prying on the steel bar to finally get it to budge. The heavy trapdoor, slowly, ever so slowly began creaking open. A hundred years of rust on those hinges finally gave way, and they slowly pulled the heavy planked trapdoor fully open. They shined their flashlights into the opening. Dust particles floated in the beams, drifting downwards into the black darkness of the abyss below the basement floor. There had been a ladder, originally. But now all that they saw were two rotted, two by fours leaning against the wall, practically crumbling into dust.

"Well we won't be using that ladder," David exclaimed.

Jerry leaned over to shine his flashlight around, down inside.

"Be careful, Grandpa," Zachary warned, "you don't want to fall in there, we'd never be able to get you out. And there could be water at the bottom."

As Jerry shined his flashlight around, he saw a door, built into the side wall of the well. The top of the door was about four feet down and the bottom of the door, about six feet below that. There was a small ledge at the bottom of the door. Jerry had an idea. "What we need is a long plank that we can stick down there and rest it on that ledge. Then we could slide down the plank to get to the door."

He took the steel bar and went over to the grain bin. "Zach and Colby, shine your lights over here," he ordered, "Dave, give me a hand here."

He began using the bar to pry loose, the top plank of the grain bin. David helped, but the old, rusted nails were tough. The plank finally came loose, but it creaked loudly and pieces of the framing that came loose with it, splintered, making a loud crackling sound.

"I hope all that noise won't wake up our upstairs residents," David commented, "although nobody is sleeping through this thunder storm."

"Let's hurry then, and get this plank down the well before we get company," Jerry ordered.

They shoved the plank down through the trap door and rested it on the ledge of the door below. Jerry hurriedly climbed down the plank. The splintered frame pieces served as cleats on the way down. When he got down to the door, he found that it was a thick oaken door, covered with a metal sheathing.

"Boy, oh boy," Jerry commented back up to the rest of his party, "those revenuers were not going to get in here."

He got out the old skeleton key that he had found in the money beer case, and tried it into the lock. His theory was correct, it fit, although it turned with difficulty in the ancient, rusty, one hundred year old lock. He had to slam his shoulder into the door several times, but finally it creaked open.

TRAPPED

IN THE HAUNTED BREW HOUSE

Just then, he heard loud voices from above, and it wasn't David or the boys. Zachary and Colby hurried down the plank. They heard the shouts again,

"Who's down here - - -, what the hell's going on down here?"

The light from flashlights shined around the room, but they couldn't see over by the well yet because it was shielded by the grain bin. David was the last one down and slammed the trap door tightly shut behind him. As he clamored down the make-shift plank ladder. he could hear the muffled voices of Billy and his partner as they called out and cursed them. The voices kept getting closer, and David heard them saying, "oh, look at the cover of the well, there's a trap door built into it, I'll bet that's where them Feiffers went, down into the well. Now we've got them."

"Oh, no you don't," David thought, "you won't get the trapdoor open without the steel bar."

But his hopes were dashed when he heard one of them say. "Oh look, I found their pry bar."

David realized he had dropped it in his panic

to get down through the trapdoor himself.

"Oh shit," he said out loud as he stepped off the plank ladder and through the steel door.

Jerry quickly closed the door and put the bar across it and locked it, just as the two evil recluses got the trap door open and came down the plank ladder. They stood outside of the steel door on the ledge and pounded on the door.

Billy yelled through the door, "Ok Feiffers, I know you're in there, and I think you may have found another one of them map circles. Why don't we talk about it? Let us in. Maybe we can split the loot this time."

"No dice, Buchanen," Jerry yelled back at him through the door. The last time we met, you threatened to kill us."

"Ok, Feiffer," Billy yelled back again. Maybe we can't get in, but you'll never get out. Later, when you're all dead, we'll come back and blow this door off and then we won't have to share the loot with you, or anyone else."

The Feiffers heard them scramble back up the plank ladder, and slam shut the trap door. Jerry turned to the group, "Looks like we won't have to worry about them for a while. So, let's check this place out."

The ancient chamber smelled only slightly musty, because it was built like a vault. The walls were concrete, about a foot thick, and so was the ceiling. There were no windows. The place was built virtually water proof and air-tight. The room was dry, and dusty smelling. It was a room about twenty five, by thirty feet in size. It was filled with mostly ancient brewing equipment.

Outside, the thunder storm rolled on across the prairie into the night. Down below, in their secret chamber, Jerry and his boys began exploring. First Jerry found a couple of the old lanterns and added kerosene from his backpack and lit the lanterns.

"Wow," David exclaimed, "no one has been in this place for a hundred years."

"It's like we're time-travelers," Zachary said

They checked out the ancient miniature brewery. In the corner on the right of the door, was the large copper pot that was the brew kettle. This old three hundred gallon vessel had a steam pipe running into it, which came from the steam boiler, which had resided on the main floor above. These steam pipes would heat and cook the brew. Next to it, there was a large coil of copper piping residing in an open-topped wooden vat that cooled the brew before it was pumped into the fermenting tanks. There were two of these against the side wall. Along the back wall, in a separate room to the cooler, were four wooden tanks where the beer was aged, or lagered. In the middle of the room there was the keg filling machine, and next to that was the bottle filler. There was a large stack of kegs at one end of the room. Alongside was a stack of beer cases. In the corner of the room, on the left of the door was a small area that looked like probably an office area. There was a desk and chair in the corner, and some shelving along one side. On the other side of the desk was a small filing cabinet and a small safe.

Jerry went straight for the office area and began going through the desk drawers. There wasn't anything of real interest in them. Most of the drawers were empty, like they had been cleaned out, except for one. Under a stack of papers, in the bottom right-hand drawer, there was a key. Jerry knew right away, what it was for. He went right over to the safe, and of course, the key fit. He opened it, and inside there was a small leather bound folio, similar to the one that he had found in the trunk. There wasn't anything else in the safe, no money of any kind. He carefully unsnapped the tab of the folio cover, and slowly opened the ancient folio. Inside there were three journal-like sheets that looked like purchase orders. Across the top of each sheet was the logo of the company. The company name was: BLACK HILLS GOLD BULLION COMPANY. on the second line: LEAD, SOUTH DAKOTA. the dates showed that they were from 1923, 1924 and 1925 There was a year-ending date on each sheet. Each purchase order was for four of the two hundred and fifty ounces of gold, at twenty dollars per ounce.

It appeared that August had traveled at the end of each year of 1923, 1924 and 1925, to Lead, South Dakota and had purchased four of the two hundred and fifty ounce gold ingots. He bought a total of twelve ingots, four in 1923, 1924 and four again in 1925. It was a well-known fact, that August didn't trust the banks in the 1920's.

But where were these ingots? There was no further paperwork or maps to show just where they might have been hidden. The old map just had a circle in the bootleg brew house. Jerry and David spent several hours going through all the papers in the file cabinet and on the book shelves, but found no further clues to the location of the gold ingots.

Zachary and Colby meanwhile began searching for another way out. They had first tried to push open the trapdoor, but found it impossible to budge. David tried it also, and then stated, "It looks like maybe Billy and his partner moved that big old gasoline engine that used to run the elevator, over onto the trapdoor."

"So, we are really trapped down here," Zachary said.

"Does that mean that what Billy said before, may come true that we are going to die down here?" Colby questioned.

"No, I don't think so," Jerry reassured him, "we may have to dig our way out, but we'll get out of here."

They finally realized that it was getting quite late. The thunder storm was passing and they could faintly hear the thunder echoing across the river valley. They also realized that they were getting very hungry , so the Feiffers all opened the backpacks and ate the lunches that they had packed. After eating, and taking a drink from their bottled spring water they began to feel sleepy, and the two young boys complained of having a slight headache.

"The air in here is starting to go bad," David said, "This place is built like a vault and is probably pretty air tight. We've got to get out of here."

"I'm just so sleepy," Colby stated, as he went over to the stack of old grain sacks in the corner and spread out several sacks and laid down on them. Zachary and David and Jerry soon followed. As the thunder rolled on in the distance, across the river valley and the lanterns burned down and went out, the Feiffer boys all fell very soundly asleep.

THE FIRST HAUNTING
1926

The Feiffers were awakened sometime later by the sound of voices and the clanging of machinery. They all sat up on their grain sack beds, but they were so groggy that they couldn't really tell if they were awake or still sleeping. They just sat there in awe at what they were seeing, or thought they were seeing, struggling to decide if they were really awake, or still sleeping and just dreaming

Franz came down the ladder and entered through the steel door. "The water in the hot water tank is at 170 degrees," he announced, "you can go ahead with the sparge."

"Ok," Joe replied, "The mash is at a reading of 1.065 gravity. I'll open the valve to start the sparge. It looks like we got the corn adjunct ratio right this time at one third volume of the mash. That bumps up our original gravity, nicely to the 1.065 range."

"So," Franz said, "That means the ABV of the batch will be around eight or nine percent. Boy, that's a lot higher than we used to brew in the old brewery before prohibition."

"Yah, that's right, Hans added from over in the corner office where he sat behind the desk doing the bookkeeping, "but it's what all the speak-easy's want these days. They say that people coming in for drinks want their alcohol and are willing to pay for it. I guess they feel they are taking the risk going there, so they want a high powered drink. Our net profit this year for the higher ABV beer is up about eighty per cent."

"Wow," Joe said, "you mean they're paying a dollar a glass for our beer, and our take is a half dollar. That's way more profitable than farming."

"Yah," Hans said, "Lewis is doing a great job selling."

"So, how much money are we making?" Franz asked.

"You know I can't tell you that, Franz," Hans replied, "because even I don't know what our quarterly totals are. Dad does those himself, and also does the banking. He has us all sworn to secrecy about all of the functions of the operation. Aside from Lewis, we don't know who the sellers or the delivery people are. He's set it up that way so that if anyone of us is arrested by the ATF officers, we can't give them anyone else's information."

"Speaking of the 'revenuers'," Joe said. "You may have noticed them coming down to the old brewery about once a month, just poking around the place to make sure nothing is being produced there anymore. I think they know that there is some beer being produced somewhere in central Minnesota, they just don't know where. I've read in the Otter Falls paper about several speak-easies being raided over by Brainerd recently."

"They came to the farm just last week," Franz said, "Joe and I were just busy feeding the hogs. It looks like our operation is pretty fool proof. There's no way for anyone to know if we are preparing a batch of hog swill in the mixing tank upstairs, or mixing a tank full of mash."

After a ten minute sparging of the mash in the tank above, Joe opened the valve and drained the wert from the mash into the brew kettle. Next, he opened the steam valve to allow the hot steam lines inside the kettle to bring the wert up to boiling temperature. The brewing phase would last one hour, with hops added at the beginning and at the last ten minutes of the brew.

As the brew was starting to boil, Joe said, "Ok boys, let's start kegging and bottling that vat of lager that's finished and ready to be sold."

Hans went to work on the kegging machine and Joe and Franz set to work on the bottling machine. Just as they were finishing the batch, August came in through the tunnel. The tunnel went out through the back wall of the basement, which was secured by another steel door, and went down the steep hillside and came out at the edge of the tamarack swamp, where a narrow water canal had been created along the edge of the swamp, obscured from view by brush and cattails and connected to the river. Canoes would come up the canal in the middle of the night, from the river, and load the bootlegged beer, to be taken down stream for distribution in towns all along the Ottertail, where there were speak-easies. It was sold all the way to Breckenridge on the Red River, and north to Moorhead and Fargo. In winter the bootleg beer was loaded onto the farm truck and covered with a load of hay, or a load of grain.

As August came in from the tunnel, Joe said to him, "We've got another batch ready to go and a new batch in the brew kettle."

"Good," August said, "Let's get this batch down to the canal for pickup tonight. When we get that done, I've got an announcement to make."

So, Joe, August, Franz and Hans began carrying the kegs and cases of the bootleg beer out the tunnel and down to the pickup spot on the canal. The shippers would be arriving soon, in their canoes at about twenty minute intervals, to haul away the bootleg stash. When they completed carrying the batch down the tunnel, they all came back in and August locked the tunnel door and turned to them.

"I've got some very bad news, boys. This may just put an end to our entire operation. I've just learned that Lewis has been arrested for selling our bootleg beer, along with his head salesman, Fred Buchanen and the owner of 'The Wild River Club', in Moorhead, one of our biggest client speak-easies. Apparently the ATF raided the speak-easy while Lewis and Fred were there delivering a shipment of our beer. I've been told that they initially escaped, but were chased all the way to Thief River Falls, where they were stopped by the local police for speeding as they came into town. The ATF officers caught up with them and arrested them. The good news, if you could call it that, is that the ATF is thinking they were selling the booze from a still and bootleg brewery in Thief River Falls. So, at least for now, we haven't been implicated."

"Looks like Lewis is going to need an attorney," Joe stated.

"Yah, I'll go up to Thief River Falls tomorrow and get one on retainer. His hearing is day after tomorrow."

"Should we go with," Franz questioned?"

"Nah, we all need to stay far away from any of those ATF boys," August stated.

So, for now, let's get the equipment scrubbed down and run that last batch out of the brew kettle and through the cooler into the fermenter. That may just be our last batch, depending on what happens to Lewis."

The Feiffer brothers finished the cleanup, and August moved the last batch into the fermenter and Joe added the yeast and cleaned the brew kettle and cooler. When finished, they all left the secret brewery chamber.

ROBB FELDER

THE SECOND HAUNTING

HIDDEN GOLD

THE END OF BOOTLEGGING

    The younger Feiffers just stared after them in shock and disbelief at what they saw, or what they dreamed they had seen. But they were still so groggy that they fell right back to sleep.

    But, again they were awakened by voices in their chamber room. This time it was August, coming in through the steel door, carrying a large satchel. He lit the lamps and went over to the desk in the office corner and got a key out of a drawer and went over to the safe and unlocked it. From it he took twelve bundles of paper money and a stack of other papers, along with the key to the steel door. He put all this into his large satchel. He reached into the safe again and pulled out two solid gold bars. He carried them over to the tunnel entrance, unlocked the door and disappeared down the tunnel. A few minutes later, he reappeared and walked over to the safe and extracted another set of the gold ingots and again disappeared into the tunnel with them. He made two more trips from safe to tunnel and returned and took out the leather folio and wrote something on the back of one of the sheets and put it back into the folio and returned the folio to the safe and locked it and put the key back in the desk drawer.

Shortly after that, they heard several large explosions, and a cloud of dust rolled out of the tunnel entrance, followed by Joe, Franz and Hans. They came in covered in dust and carrying several sacks of cement.

"Well, we blew up the tunnel," Joe announced, "all the way from just past the chimney base, down to the swamp."

"Ok, that's good, boys," August said, "Now while I make a run with the last of our cash, you three can mix up the cement and seal up the tunnel entrance. When I get back I'll lock up and hide the key. Who knows if we'll ever be able to operate this brewery again. Those damn Revenuers are breathing down our necks after they arrested Lewis and Fred Buchanen. When I was at their trial where they were sentenced to five years in prison for selling bootleg beer, the ATF boys were hanging out there and questioned me about my possible connection to Lewis and Fred. I of course denied any connection, other than Lewis was my son. But they're a pretty suspicious bunch, and I have a feeling they'll be checking us out pretty closely for a while. That's why we're shutting down the operation. It's just not worth it anymore. I don't want anyone else going to jail for selling or making bootleg. I've collected the last of our take on that last run and paid up all the shippers and

MYSTERY ON THE OTTER TAIL

sellers."

With that, August left through the steel door and up the ladder and through the trap door with the satchel. Just as he entered the basement, he heard voices outside and the sound of a car engine idling. He knew right away from the sound of the engine, that it was one of those big V8 engines in one of those ATF pursuit cars. He stuck his head back down into the trapdoor and said to his sons, "The ATF boys are outside. Lock up and bolt the door and stay put until I get back. I'm going to make a run for it with this money, down along the river and hide it somewhere."

With that, August closed the trapdoor and hurried out the back basement door of the granary and ran down the hill in the darkness, and down along the river bank. The ATF agents entered the main floor of the hog slop kitchen and yelled, asking if anyone was there. Down below in the basement, Joe, Franz and Hans stopped their cementing and quietly waited. August made his way down the river bank to the old brewery bottling plant and entered the basement door. He made his way to the back and grabbed an empty beer case on his way to the back room where the now empty beer storage vat was. He hurriedly stashed all the bundles of cash into the old beer case, along with the paperwork and the key. He took the beer case and stashed it into the empty beer vat and closed it up securely. He hurried out of the basement and made his way quickly to the farmhouse, just as the ATF car was pulling up in front. Two agents came to the door and August answered. They showed him their badges.

"We were just at your hog barn," the lead agent said.

"Yeah, so," August replied, "I saw you drive in."

"We want to ask you a couple of questions about your hog operation."

"My hogs are none of your damn business," August said.

"Well it's not about just the hogs," the agent said, "we noticed that water tank and steam boiler. Looks like it came from a brewery or maybe a still."

"I bought those when you guys closed down the old brewery. Do you want to see my receipt?"

"No, no, that won't be necessary," the agent replied. But why do you need a steam boiler?"

"We have steam lines that run out into the hog barn to keep the feed troughs from freezing in the winter. It gets cold here in Minnesota. Where you guys from, Florida or someplace? Come back next winter and I'll treat you to some nice warm swill."

"Well, we did test your swill that was left in the mixing tank and it checked out okay, no mashing converted sugars."

"Yah, it's just ground oats and barley and water, kinda like oatmeal. Ya want to take a bucket of it home with you for breakfast?"

"Now, don't be a smart ass," the agent

replied, "where are your three sons?"

"They're probably over in the cattle barn doing chores. Did you think to look there?"

"Well, no," the agent replied.

"So, now who's the dumb ass," August asked? "Ya know, I'm pretty damn sick and tired of you guys coming, snooping around here every time you don't have anything better to do. I've been very cooperative so far, just letting you waltz in here any old time of day or night. You've been through the old brewery a dozen times so far this year. That building is now personal property you know. So from now on, your little party is over. I don't want to see your ugly faces on my property again, unless you have a warrant. Got it? You just quit harassing me and my family or I'll file charges on you for searching without cause or a warrant. Now good night, get the hell off my property."

As he slammed the door, Annie came over to him and said, "That sounded like a pretty heated discussion. What's going, on August?"

"Oh, those damn Feds. won't leave us alone. I mean just because we live next to a shuttered brewery, they seem to think somehow, that we're still making beer here, especially after Lewis got in trouble for selling bootleg beer up in Moorhead.

"I know," Annie said, "I feel so bad for Lewis and his friend Fred, getting sentenced to five years in prison after the owner of that speak-easy in Moorhead double-crossed them and ratted on them, then testified against them at their trial"

August just hung his head, feeling very guilty, but he couldn't express any of his guilt to Annie, because she knew absolutely nothing about her husband and son's bootleg business. So he just said that he agreed with her that their son Lewis got a really bad deal. As he turned away, he said he was going out to the barn to help their other sons with the chores.

He walked slowly to the barnyard, he was deep in thought and guilt for what had happened. He was extremely grateful to Lewis for not exposing his bootleg operations. Now they would have to turn their focus to the farming operation and try to completely forget about bootlegging. They had made a huge amount of money, but now they wouldn't be able to spent any of it. The ATF would be monitoring their bank accounts, so the money and gold would have to remain hidden, for the foreseeable future.

Later August would draw up a map with clues to where the illegal money and gold was hidden. "Maybe, sometime in the future, or even some future generation would be able to find the loot," he thought.

"All this, just because I wanted to keep on brewing beer, I've brewed beer my entire life. I started back in Heidleberg, Germany, at my dad's brewery. And now this Prohibition thing. What a lot of nonsense. People have been brewing beer for about six thousand years, starting in ancient Babylon and Egypt. Now our government thinks they are going to stop it. They're fools, those damn politicians for listening to those 'do-gooders' temperance crazies. It won't last. There's almost as much booze being made today illegally as there was legal booze before Prohibition. People want their booze and that's all there's to it. People have to make up their own mind if they want to drink or not."

When he got to the farmyard, he went into the granary basement and through the trapdoor, down the well and unlocked the steel door and went into the secret chamber. Joe, Franz and Hans were just finishing, sealing up the tunnel entrance.

"Good job," he told them, "why don't you boys go over to the cattle barn and get the chores done. I will finish closing everything down and locking up."

The Feiffer brothers left as August checked everything over, making sure the water and steam lines were shut down. He double checked everything and then left through the steel door and locked it. He took his copy of the key, and in a very sad and depressed mood, he dropped the key down into the bottom of the well, never to be found and used again. He climbed out the trapdoor and closed it securely, and threw a thick layer of dust over it. Little did he know, although he suspected, - - - no one would enter the secret brewery chamber for over a hundred years.

ROBB FELDER

BACK TO THE FUTURE

DISCOVERING THE GOLD

The next generation of Feiffers stared in disbelief as August left the chamber and locked the steel door. They were sitting upright now almost fully awake, albeit, still a little groggy and hardly believing what they had just seen in their almost 'dream-hallucinogenic' state. As they slowly became more conscious and awake, they all were experiencing headaches.

"We've got to get out of here," David said, "the air is getting worse, the longer we stay."

"I know, I agree," Jerry replied, "but we can't go back up through the trapdoor."

"Well, let's find that secret entrance to the tunnel," Zachary said.

"Yeah, maybe we can bust through where they sealed it up," Colby added, "We've got picks and shovels in our backpacks."

So they went over behind the ancient brew kettle and found the sealed up entrance. They immediately went to work, Jerry and David began chipping into the mortar lines between the stones, and Zachary and Colby shoveled the debris out of the way. They worked for about an hour and were almost through the blockage, when they decided to take a break. They drank some water, as Zachary said, "I wish we had packed some Tylenol for this headache."

"Me too," Colby said, 'now my stomach is getting upset too."

"Well, we should break through the seal very soon, and hopefully there will be some fresher air in the tunnel. That should help these headaches," Jerry said, "and from there we can break through to the outside."

"So let's get back to work," David said, "we can do this."

They all went back to work, picking and shoveling. In a few minutes they broke through into the tunnel. The air was a little fresher in the tunnel, and their headaches subsided a little. They soon had a hole large enough to crawl through. The tunnel section behind the seal wasn't very long before it ended again at the collapsed section and was strewn with debris from the explosion that had collapsed the rest of the tunnel. The open section was about ten feet long and ran just past the old chimney base. The Feiffers went to work and piled up enough of the debris for them to reach the ceiling, where they soon had a hole punched through large enough to crawl out through. They all took deep breaths of the cool fresh nighttime air. Jerry cautioned them to be quiet though, "We still have those upstairs residents in the granary to worry about."

"Well, let's get back to camp," Colby whispered, "I'm still tired and very hungry."

Hold on," Jerry said, "There's something we need to check out before we leave. Dave, you come with me back down into the tunnel. Zach and Colby, you guys stand guard up here in case Billy shows up."

When they were back inside the tunnel, Jerry said to David, "I just remembered what one of the clues said that was written on the map. It said 'one and three are yellow, and black as soot'."

Jerry went over to the section of the tunnel wall that ran past the old chimney. There in the wall, was a small steel door that had been installed as a 'clean-out' door for the chimney. He opened the door and a cloud of soot drifted out onto the floor. The soot had probably not been cleaned out in a very, very long time. He shined his flashlight into the opening. There appeared to be about a foot of soot in the base of the chimney. He took his shovel and began shoveling the soot out onto a pile on the tunnel floor. He scraped the chimney floor clear of soot, but saw nothing. Jerry was just about to give up his search when he shined his flashlight into the space and discovered a loose brick in the floor of the chimney base. He used his pick to pry it up, then another, and another. Finally there was an opening about two feet square in the floor. He shined his flashlight again into the floor opening. Down in the hole was an old beer keg. He couldn't lift it out. It was too heavy, however, the top was loose, so he pried it off. There, inside the beer keg was a stack of what looked like bricks, wrapped in wax paper. He lifted one out. It was very heavy. He peeled back the wax paper. It wasn't a brick exactly, but a brick of solid gold. He counted eight of them. Jerry handed the first one to David, then another, and said, "Hand these up to the boys and tell him to put them in his backpack."

He got another two bricks out and said to hand those to the other boy to put in his backpack.

"We've got to get these out of here," He said to David as he handed him two more for his backpack, "before Billy gets in here and discovers these."

Jerry put the last two gold bricks into his backpack, then removed the beer keg as well. He had a plan for it. As David handed it up to the boys, Jerry closed the small steel clean-out door. Both he and David climbed up out of the tunnel, although it was quite difficult with the extra weight in their back packs. When they were out, Jerry said, "Now, we've got to cover the hole that we made into the tunnel."

So they carefully and quietly covered the hole, and any evidence that they had escaped. The Feiffers then donned their heavy backpacks and made their way carefully down the hillside over the rubble of the blasted, caved in tunnel to the edge of the tamarack swamp. Jerry and David took turns carrying the beer keg. They went around the edge of the swamp to where the swamp met the river's edge. There they climbed to the bluff overlooking the swamp and river, where there was a high point of the river bank. Here Jerry found a very large oak tree that grew out of the edge of the river bluff. Some of the large roots of the giant oak tree were exposed by erosion over the eons of time. Here, between the large roots of the giant oak tree, they began digging a small but quite deep hole. It was about two feet square, by about five feet deep. Into it, Jerry first placed the beer keg and next, he placed all eight of the heavy gold ingots inside the keg, and put the lid on it. They covered their treasure and closed the hole and heaped a number of large rocks on top of it amongst the large tree roots.

As they were hiking back up the river toward their camp, they suddenly heard voices coming down the trail toward them. They quickly ducked into the thick brush in one of the wash-outs. In the early dawn twilight, they observed Billy Buchanen and his partner, Frank, pass by on the trail carrying the old beer case with the worthless money in it. But just as Billy got past where the Feiffers were hiding, Jerry moved a bit and stepped on a dried old twig, that snapped loudly. Billy and Frank set down the beer case.

Billy said, "Did you hear that?"

The duo drew their guns and crept into the wash-out where the Feiffers had been hiding. But the Feiffers were already running through the brush, up the gully. Billy and Frank began shooting after them, but couldn't really make out who, or, what it was that made the noise. In the twilight, and the thick brush. they decided not to pursue whoever, or whatever had run away.

"Billy said to his partner, "Hold your fire. Its probably just a couple deer."

"Yeah," his partner said, "it wouldn't have been them Feiffers. We've got them locked up in the basement. I guess we're just a little jumpy, after raiding their camp."

When Jerry, David and the boys arrived back at their camp, they found that it had been totally decimated. Their tent and sleeping bags had been ripped apart and thrown into the fire. The camp tables were busted up and in the fire. The camp stove was smashed on a rock. Their fishing gear had been tossed into the river. One of the canoes had been smashed, and pieces of it were also in the fire. The other canoe was swamped and at the bottom of the river, along with the coolers of fish..

"Why don't you, Zach and Colby, get the canoe and the coolers up from the bottom of the river?" David said, "It looks like those are the only things we can salvage. Then we may as well pack up anything else that's salvageable, which isn't much, and get out of here."

"Yeah, we obviously can't stay here any longer," Jerry said, "We may as well head for home."

So while the boys pulled the canoe up from the river bottom, Jerry and David called home to let everyone know that they were coming back. When asked why they hadn't called for two days, they were totally taken aback, but replied that they had experienced a very severe thunder storm that pretty well destroyed their camp and made it impossible to call out.

After the call, Jerry and Dave just looked at each other, in shock, for a moment. So," David said, questioning no one in particular, "This is Friday? That means we were locked in that secret chamber for two days, not just overnight."

They all just stared at each other for a moment, trying to process that thought. Finally Zachary said, "I just can't believe that we slept for two whole days."

"It must have been the bad air in the chamber," David said.

"Yeah," Jerry said, "They say depleted oxygen can do strange things to the brain. We were lucky to get out of there alive."

When the canoe was ready, they put out the fire, and dug a big hole in the sand and cleaned up their campsite and buried all the debris. They loaded the coolers and their backpacks into the canoe. They all four got into the one remaining canoe and began paddling downstream, heading for their truck under the highway bridge. It was slow going because they were really overloaded. They passed under the railroad bridge and pulled ashore under the highway bridge, where they loaded the canoe and what was left of their gear into the truck.

Just as they were about to pull up the river bank and out onto the highway, that notorious brown, rusty Chevy truck pulled off the highway and stopped right in front of them. The two evil villains got out with guns drawn

"Well, well," Billy said, "What have we here? Are you leaving so soon? Damn, I thought we had you locked up in that basement. I suppose you dug your way out. OK Feiffers, where's the gold? I know you must have it."

"There's no gold Billy," Jerry replied, "And thanks to you destroying our camp, we were just heading home."

"Well, I just don't believe you," Billy said, "So get out of the truck and show me your hands, and no funny stuff with the knives this time, or somebody gets shot."

So the Feiffers got out, and Billy said, "Ok, get down on the ground while we search your truck. I'm pretty sure there's gold in there. I know about the gold Feiffer. You see, my stepdad was in prison with your uncle Lewis. Lewis told him about the gold."

As the two villains were bent over, with their heads into the truck, looking under the seats, Jerry and David quickly got up and very quietly grabbed two of the shovels from the back of the truck. They crept up behind the two, and when they raised up their heads, Jerry and David both swung their shovels and clobbered them on the back of their heads. The two fell to the ground, out cold.

MYSTERY ON THE OTTER TAIL

Jerry yelled, "Everyone, get back in the truck."

He got behind the wheel and ripped around the brown Chevy truck, and the two recluses left lying on the ground. They got out onto the highway and sped away.

About a mile or two down the road however, Jerry saw, in his rearview mirror, the brown Chevy truck coming up rapidly behind them.

"Oh damn," David said, "We forgot to get their guns."

Jerry accelerated and stayed ahead of the brown Chevy, but the Chevy was still on their tail, about a hundred yards back. Suddenly the Feiffers heard several loud 'pops', followed by the sound of bullets whizzing by the windows . More loud pops and they heard the bullets thumping into the tailgate. Suddenly Jerry felt a very sharp pain in his left shoulder and cried out, as a bullet tore into his upper arm, stopping at his shoulder joint. Luckily, the bullet had lost a lot of its momentum when it passed through the truck body.

"Are you okay Grandpa?" Colby questioned.

"Yeah, I think so," Jerry replied, "I just got nicked by one of the bullets. Probably just a flesh wound."

As Jerry accelerated all he could, he saw, in his rearview mirror, the flashing red lights of a highway patrol car coming up behind the brown Chevy. The Chevy slowed and pulled over, and so did Jerry. As he walked back to the Chevy and the patrol car, the two highway patrolmen already had both Billy and Frank out of the truck and leaning over the hood of the patrol car. The patrolman asked Jerry if he was in some kind of a race with Billy.

"No, no, "Jerry replied, "He was chasing me and shooting at me."

"I was not," Billy denied, "I don't even have a gun."

"Well they probably threw them out when they saw the flashing red lights behind them," Jerry said, "Come, look at the back of my truck and see where they hit my truck."

The patrolman handcuffed the two, and put them into the patrol car. One of the patrolman walked up the road to Jerrys truck, and the other patrolman walked back down the highway and began looking for the guns. The patrolman looked at Jerrys tailgate and said, "Yup, you were definitely shot at."

As Jerry turned, the patrolman noticed the hole in his shirt, and the blood soaking through in an ever growing circle, and Jerry could feel the blood starting to trickle down his arm.

"Hey, what's that?" the patrolman asked. "Looks like you took a hit yourself."

He led Jerry back to his patrol car and got his first-aid kit, and had Jerry lay over the trunk of the car while he applied a pressure bandage to his shoulder wound.

"There, that should slow the bleeding until you get to an ER. There's one in Wadena, the next town up the highway. But you'd better let someone else drive you there. I don't want you driving with that wound."

The patrolman took pictures of Jerry's wound and his truck, as the other patrolman came from the other direction with the two guns in an evidence bag, and took the two perpetrators back out of the patrol car. The lead patrolman told Billy and his accomplice, "You are under arrest for assault with a deadly weapon, discharging a firearm on a US highway and possession of an unregistered firearm." The patrolman read Billy and his friend their rights, and as he was putting the two back into the patrol car, Billy yelled at Jerry, "This ain't over, Feiffer, that's my gold, and I aim to get it."

"What gold is he talking about?" the patrolman asked Jerry.

"I have no idea," Jerry replied, "that guy is just half crazy."

The patrolman took some more information from Jerry and told him to be prepared to appear in court for the hearing and trial of the two. Jerry walked back to his truck and got in. As he pulled the truck back onto the highway, everyone was silent for a while. They were all probably still in shock after being shot at.

Finally Colby exclaimed, "wow, that was a close call. Thank goodness for those patrolmen. Who knows what would have happened if they hadn't come along."

When they got to the exit for the town of

Wadena, Jerry pulled off and followed the signs to the hospital ER. A doctor opened the bandage that the patrolman put on Jerry's bullet wound, gave Jerry a shot of Novocain and dug out the bullet. They didn't ask too many questions, because the patrolman had already called the hospital with the information. When they got back to the truck, Jerry finally let David drive the rest of the way home.

"But what are you going to tell Grandma Barb?" Zachary questioned, "about the bullet holes in your truck, Grandpa, and that shoulder wound."

"I don't know, I guess I'll have to start explaining everything to her. I know she won't be too happy about it. I'll probably have a hard time getting away again for a while, to do any more exploring for those other map circles, or even to retrieve those gold bars."

"Well, you may have to get a new crew for your next expedition," David said, "I can't get any more time off this year, and the boys both have summer jobs starting next week."

"I don't want you boys telling your friends, or anyone else about our little exploration and discovery of the gold. After all, it was indeed a fishing trip, and we have the fish to prove it. So just let the rest ride, at least until we see how this thing with Billy plays out. I will probably have to go back to Otter Falls for Billy and Frank's hearing and trial, in the coming weeks. I'll more than likely be subpoenaed as a material witness."

"What about all that gold?" Zachary

questioned.

"I just don't know yet," Jerry replied, Even if we can get back there to dig it up, it's very difficult to cash in that much gold."

They drove the rest of the way back in silence. Each of them deep in thought about the gold, and about the whole week of adventure, filled with danger and discovery. When they got to Jerry's house, Barbara came running out to greet them. "I'm so glad to see all of you back, safe and sound. I was so worried about you when Grandpa told me about the terrible storm you guys had up there,"

"I know," Colby said, "Our camp was destroyed, and we lost one of our canoes, but we salvaged all our fish, and we caught a lot of fish."

They divided up the fish, and David and the boys left for home. Jerry had to run over to the sporting goods rental store and explain about the busted up canoe and pay for it. He returned home and began the process of explaining everything to Barbara. She checked his shoulder wound and said, "No more of this nonsense. You could have been killed."

ROBB FELDER

BOOK TWO

ROBB FELDER

RETURN AGAIN

TO OTTER FALLS

BATTLE FOR THE GOLD

Ten days after returning home, Jerry got a notice to appear in the Otter Falls county court for a hearing of the charges against Billy Buchanen and Frank Klienbacher. At the hearing, Jerry appeared for the prosecution. The county attorney presented the charges against Billy and Frank and a statement from Jerry, along with pictures of the bullet holes in the tailgate of his truck. Jerry also presented his record of treatment of a gunshot wound to his left shoulder from the Wadena hospital ER.

Billy and Frank pleaded not guilty. Billy and Frank's defense attorney stated that Billy was employed as a security guard for the Lakes and Land Company, which still owned the property. and that the Feiffers were trespassing. The county prosecutor argued that the Feiffers were just fishing on the river, which is public domain, and Billy had no cause to pursue the Feiffers and fire weapons at them on a US highway.

The judge ordered that the two perpetrators should stand trial and set a trial date of November fifteenth. He set bail at fifty thousand dollars.

After the hearing, Jerry went to a sporting goods rental store in Otter Falls and rented a canoe and headed to the Ottertail River bridge again. First he stopped at a restaurant in town and had dinner. After he finished eating, he called Barbara and told her that the hearing ran late and that he was staying in Otter Falls for the night.

He parked his old Ford truck under the bridge again. He unloaded the canoe and as the sun was setting, he paddled quietly up the river. He found a spot on the opposite side of the river from the ancient brewery ruins and just across from the high point of the bank that separated the tamarack swamp from the river. He pulled his canoe up into some thick brush and made a small campsite out of sight from the river. There would be no campfire or tent here tonight, just a sleeping bag on the ground under his overturned canoe. Here he waited and slept until well after midnight. He took one of his backpacks with only a small shovel and carefully waded across the river, with only the faint light from a sliver of a moon to see by. Fortunately the water was only about knee-deep where he was crossing. On the other side, he slowly and carefully climbed the steep bank up to the large old oak tree. Jerry carefully removed the stones they had placed over the keg with the gold inside. He began digging down between the tree roots, just as he and his boys had done earlier. He found the keg undisturbed and began loading the gold bars into his backpack. His wounded left shoulder was really hurting after all the digging, so he decided to only take two bars at a time. This meant four trips across the river in the faint moonlight. After he had removed the last two bars, he covered up the old keg and hole under the big oak tree and replaced the rocks and made his way back across the river for the final time, to his campsite. He put four bars each in his two backpacks and crawled into his sleeping bag under the canoe and fell asleep rapidly. He was exhausted from all the digging, climbing the steep bank and wading back and forth across the river multiple times. He slept soundly, but awoke with a start with the morning sun in his eyes and the sound of a truck, - - that truck, in the distance. "That damn old rusty brown Chevy truck again," He thought. That could mean only one thing, - - Billy and Frank had somehow made bail."

    Jerry quickly loaded the two very heavy backpacks into the canoe and took off downstream as fast as possible. He hoped that he could beat Billy and Frank to the bridge. As he rounded the back side of the island, he kept to the side of the river, moving slowly through the cattails until he could see the highway bridge up ahead. He pulled his canoe to a stop. There, under the bridge, parked next to his truck was the old rusty brown Chevy truck of Billy's. He stopped for a long time, hidden in the cattails, trying to figure out what to do. Finally, he had a plan. He carefully took each backpack full of the gold bars, tied a rope on them and lowered them slowly and quietly into the shallow muddy water beneath a large clump of the cattails. No one but him would know they were there, and it would be temporary. He was only about a hundred yards from the bridge. Jerry patiently waited for a train to cross the railroad bridge. The noise would mask any sound he might make as he carefully backed his canoe out of the cattail cluster and out into the main stream of the river. He proceeded downstream, under the railroad bridge and pulled ashore under the highway bridge where he knew his nemesis, Billy awaited him. As he stepped ashore, Billy approached him with a gun in hand again.

"Well, well, Feiffer, looks like we meet again. Ya know, we've got to stop meeting so often, people will start to talk," Billy said as he snickered at his own attempt at humor.

"Now, I know damn well you've struck gold, Feiffer, and I aim to find where you've hidden it."

"And, I keep telling ya, Buchanen, there ain't no gold."

This statement really angered Billy, and he rushed at Jerry and 'pistol-whipped' him on the side of his head. This knocked Jerry to the ground with a bloody ear.

"Don't mess with me, Feiffer, I should just kill you now."

"You just do that," Jerry replied, "and you'll never find your damn gold." He had to make this look real, to set the trap for Billy and Frank.

Billy rushed again at Jerry as he lay on the ground holding his bloody ear, as Billy attempted to kick Jerry in the gut. But Jerry caught his boot and pulled him off balance. As he fell backward, he fired his gun, but the shot went up into the bottom of the bridge decking.

Billy regained his balance and again aimed his weapon at Jerry and yelled, "Alright Feiffer, I'm going to shoot you right now."

"No, no," Jerry yelled, "I'll tell you where the damn gold is. It's not worth anyone's life."

"Alright then, Feiffer, but this better be good, or you're a dead man."

"I stashed the gold at the bottom of the big spring, up the river. It's in a gunny-sack at the end of a twenty foot rope tied to a log in the mouth of the spring."

"Ok Feiffer, here's how we're going to do this. I will go up to the big spring and get my gold. You will stay here with Frank. If I come back with gold, you live and we part ways for good, if no gold, you die and Frank will dig your grave right here under this bridge , maybe over there right next to your damn Ford truck."

"Ok, deal," Jerry said. But he knew that would never happen. Even if he had put the gold in the spring, Billy would either come back and kill him and Frank, or just take off for Mexico, with the gold and leave him and Frank to just figure it out, or kill each other.

MYSTERY ON THE OTTER TAIL

THE CONFESSION

Billy gave his gun to Frank and said, "If he moves, shoot him."

"And I will shoot you," Frank said, "Just like I did to your uncle Lewis, after he made that crappy deal to sell the farm to that cheese company back in 1983."

"Yes, he did," confirmed Billy, "After we tried for days to get the location of the gold out of him. He double-crossed us, you know. My stepdad and him were in prison together back in the twenties, for that bootlegging wrap. He told my stepdad, in prison, that there was some of the bootleg loot hidden in the old brewery, along with gold that your Grandpa August bought because he didn't trust the banks."

"That's right," Frank continued, "After I shot him, we dumped his body down the well in the old farmhouse, along with that folio full of worthless papers he claimed were from his 'special side-deal' he made for fifty grand for the brewery. Then we burned that house down and claimed that Lewis did it, and that he ran off, back to California with the money."

With that, Billy jumped into his rusty brown Chevy truck and took off to go up the river, to the big spring. After he left, Jerry slowly struggled to his feet and said to Frank, "Would you give me a hand loading my canoe into my truck so I can leave as soon as Billy gets back with the gold."

"Load your own damn canoe, Feiffer," Frank said. "When Billy gets back, he's going to kill you anyway. I may as well kill you now and save him the trouble."

"Do you really think Billy's going to share his gold with anyone after all he's been through to get it. My bet is that if he does come back with the gold, he will just kill us both. Or he may not come back at all. He'll just take off with the gold for Mexico. You know there's a lot more gold to be found in the old brewery ruins, and Billy's not going to share the gold from the spring with you. Have you ever even seen the map where the gold is located in the ruins?"

"Well, no," Frank replied, "Billy ain't never showed me no map."

"I have a copy right here," Jerry said, as he started to pick up the canoe. Frank climbed down off of a cement section of the bridge abutment where he had been sitting and holding the gun on Jerry. As Frank came over towards where Jerry was standing holding the canoe, he stumbled a bit on some of the loose rocks on the shore. That was just the opening Jerry was hoping for. With perfect timing he swung the canoe around and knocked Frank over backwards. He fell back and struck his head on the cement section of the bridge abutment. He was out cold. Jerry set the canoe

MYSTERY ON THE OTTER TAIL

back down and carefully went over to him to make sure he was knocked out and not dead. This time, he picked up the gun. Next, he got a section of rope from the canoe and tied up Frank, but not too securely. He got back into his canoe and paddled like crazy, back up to the clump of cattails and retrieved the backpacks with the gold bars. He got back under the bridge and loaded the gold into his truck, and also the canoe, and the gun. Then he got a piece of paper and pencil from his truck glove box and drew a map of the old brewery and farm basements. He drew a couple of circles on it but, where not the same as the original map. He put a circle in the old smoke house, and another in the old malt kiln. He wrote some random numbers in the circles that had no meaning whatsoever. He took and rubbed some mud on the map and some tears around the edges, to make it look authentic. He laid it out on one of his empty backpacks with a rock on top of it, just as Frank was coming too. Jerry told Frank that if he hurried and got loose before Billy got back, he could take the map and start looking for his own gold.

Jerry hurried and climbed into the truck before Billy showed up. He made a bee-line for the bank in Otter Falls and stashed four of the gold bars in his safe deposit box. Next, he returned the canoe and sleeping bag to the sports shop. He got gas for his truck and headed for home. But, he went back by a different highway, just in case he would be followed. All the way back to the cities, he kept checking his rear-view mirrors to make sure he didn't have any followers. He was incredibly tense all the way. Who wouldn't be, with about a million dollars worth of gold bars in his truck. When he got back into the cities, he first went to his regular bank and rented a safe deposit box and stashed two more of the gold bars in it. Next he went to a Wells Fargo bank and rented a safe deposit box there, and stashed the last two of the gold bars.

THE TRIAL

THE HUNT

AND

HALLOWEEN

Summer was melting away; from the hot sunny days of July into the hazy, humid days of August. Barbara and Jerry had finally sold their house and were moving into their new senior housing apartment. It had been a difficult struggle, downsizing all their belongings to fit the much smaller living space. But they had accomplished it. Now, as the last hazy days of summer slowly faded into the cooler clearer days of September, they were trying to adjust to their new life style. All of their grandchildren were now in college and all the great grandkids back at school. The long hot days of summer slowly faded into the crisper days of autumn. The beautiful brilliant color of autumn leaves faded and fell into huge piles of leaves everywhere, and the chilly west wind swept them into every nook and cranny of everyone's yard. Jerry and Barbara were so glad that for once they didn't have to dig the leaves out of every corner and crevasse of their yard. Yard work was a thing of the past for this couple. Now it was a time to relax and enjoy the maintenance free living that everyone looks forward to, right? - - -. Well, not exactly for this still 'type-a' couple. By early October, Jerry was pacing the floor, looking for some kind of activity to occupy his time. Barbara was adjusting quite well. She was busy with sewing, quilting and other handwork. She had joined several quilting clubs. She also volunteered at the church and hospital.

Finally, she said to Jerome, "you know, you have that trial coming up for Billy and Frank on the fifth of November.

"Yah," Jerry replied, "I'm really not looking forward to it. These guys are employed by that damn cheese company and that company will provide them with some pretty good lawyers."

"Well, none the less, you have been subpoenaed, so you'll have to be there. But I don't want you to go by yourself this time. And I want you to stay away from that damn brewery. That place is just too dangerous. I was worried sick about you last time. You nearly got yourself killed by that maniac, Billy. You know, I'd come with you, but I just can't get someone to sub for me at the hospital. They are just too short-staffed right now."

"Yeah, I know Barb, honey, but look at all the money and gold we've gotten so far. We have enough for the rest of our lives, and to put our grandkids through college."

"But, what good is it all, if you get yourself killed by that crazy psychopath Frank."

"Yah, you're right about that for sure. Well, I've talked to my sister Mary, and she's agreed to go with me to the trial. And there will be a lot of deer hunters out along the river woods. I've talked to our son Bob, and he said he would like to try deer hunting up there this year. So, maybe we could just blend in with all the other hunters."

"That's true, and now that you've finally got yourself a new Ford truck, you will be less conspicuous than that old Ford you had."

"Yah," Jerry thought, "And maybe if we're equipped for hunting, we'll have some protection from those two crazies guarding the old place."

As the trial date approached, Jerry and his son Bob prepared for the hunt. The weather in North Central Minnesota after the first of November can turn into winter in a hurry. They both made sure their winter clothing was up to date. Because they hadn't hunted in several years, they had to upgrade several clothing items. New boots were bought, as well as caps and mittens. Of course, the deer rifles were checked, sighted, cleaned and oiled.

Just about the time they thought they were equipped and ready, Jerry got requests from some of the grandkids to go along on the hunting trip. Ellen, Brittany, Ryan and Luke wanted to go. Jerry said okay, so they made arrangements to take several days off college and work. Jerry and Bob had extra deer hunting rifles. This trip, they wouldn't be camping, of course, so Jerry made reservations for three rooms at The Otter Motel in Otter Falls. He took the grandkids out shopping for their blaze orange hunting clothes. Thankfully they wouldn't have to pack a lot of food, just enough in their backpacks for the daytime hunt. They all also picked up their hunting licenses at Fleet Farm. They also packed picks and shovels, of course for more exploring of the ancient brewery ruins. Lastly, Jerry had to call the Lakes and Land Company to get permission to hunt on what was still company land along the Ottertail River. He was told it was ok to hunt on the old Feiffer farm. They had already given permission to a couple of other hunters.

"But stay away from the old brewery," he was warned, "It's become so dangerous that we're going to have to level it. And with our original guards, Billy and Frank arrested on criminal charges, we just can't afford to replace them. There'll really be nothing left to guard."

An icy drizzle began to fall as Jerry's troop began checking into their motel in Otter Falls. It was very late in October. In fact, tomorrow would be Halloween. Deer hunting season was still almost a week away. They were here early. The trial was still about two weeks out. However, Jerry had received a notice for a pre-trial hearing on the morning of October thirty first. So, rather than make multiple trips back and forth from the

Twin Cities, the kids agreed that they could use the extra time to scout the woods looking for deer signs. They got checked into their three separate rooms, Bob and Luke took one room, Ellen and Brittany had another room, and Jerry and Ryan took the third room. After the long drive and a nice big dinner, they all crashed early.

The morning was again icy cool, and the drizzle was still falling. They all met in the motel lobby after breakfast.

"You guys all dress warm and dry," Jerry said, "It looks like this icy drizzle is going to last all day."

"Yah, it's going to be a mess in the woods today," Bob said, "We'll wear our rain coats and hunting boots and try to keep our feet dry."

"Let's all meet back here for lunch and hopefully this drizzle will let up so we can do some exploring this afternoon, at the old farmhouse."

"Good luck with your pre-trial hearing, Grandpa," Ellen said.

"Yeah, good luck, I hope they nail those guys good for what they did to you last spring." Ryan said.

Bob and the young hunters headed out in Bob's truck with their deer stands and rain gear. Because the deer season was still a week away, they didn't have to wear blaze orange clothing yet. Jerry warned them to stay away from the brewery and farm building ruins, so they headed for the large woods along the river at the top end of the old Feiffer farm, north of the big spring. This was, in fact, the very same woods that, over one hundred years ago, a previous generation of young Feiffer's had met the Indian hunters, who had saved their lives by shooting that huge black bear. Jerry, meantime, headed over to the courthouse where he met up with his sister, Mary.

"Thanks for coming with me to this hearing, Sis," Jerry said, "No one likes to appear in court alone. No matter which side you are on."

"Amen to that, Brother," Mary said, "You said there were some new developments that will be discussed today. Let's go in and find out if they are favorable."

The hearing was held in a conference room. Present were; the county prosecutor, along with Jerry and Mary, the defense attorney and, Billy and Frank. The judge called the hearing to order. The court reporter began taking notes. The defense attorney stated that they had reached an agreement on a plea deal. The prosecutor agreed and read the terms of the agreement. Billy and frank would plead guilty to the charge of discharging a firearm on a US highway and possession of an unregistered firearm, a misdemeanor. The charge of assault with a deadly weapon, a felony, would be dropped. The judge imposed a sentence of two years of probation, and they could not possess a firearm for two years.

After the hearing, Billy and Frank came up to Jerry and Mary on the steps of the courthouse.

"I still want my damn gold, Feiffer," Billy proclaimed.

"And I'm still telling you, there isn't any gold, Buchanen," Jerry replied.

"Then why'd ya give me that map, Feiffer?" Frank questioned.

"Well, if you think there's gold in that damn old brewery, then you'll just have to find it yourselves."

With that, they parted company. On their way back to their cars, Mary said to Jerry, "Boy, all this talk about gold in that old place, sure makes me wonder if maybe there really was some gold hidden in there."

"Well. I'll let you know what I find."

"You be careful, Jerry, that Billy and Frank sure look like a dangerous pair. Good luck hunting next week. But you tell those young people to watch out for that Billy and Frank pair. And be careful driving. The weather people are predicting a drop in temperature and with this drizzle continuing, could result in a really bad ice storm, maybe even our first snowfall."

"Thanks for the warning, Sis, and thanks again for coming with me to court. I'll keep you posted on the gold situation. Say hi to Heinrich and the boys."

It was almost lunch time, so Jerry headed back to the motel. A short time later he was joined by the rest of his crew. At lunch, they all discussed their morning, and made plans for the afternoon.

"So, how did it look for deer signs in that woods north of the springs?' Jerry questioned.

"It looks very promising," Bob replied, "We found some very good deer runs. Go ahead, girls, tell Grandpa what you found."

"Brittany and I found a real heavily traveled trail on the north end of the woods," Ellen said.

"Yeah, it looks like the trail goes up from the lower woods, along the river and runs up a short washout, up the hill and out onto the prairie hay fields," Brittany said.

"It looks like the deer feed on the prairie hays at night, then return down this trail into the thick brush along the river swamp to bed down during the day," Ellen said. We're going to set up our deer stands along this trail."

"How about you guys?" Jerry questioned Luke and Ryan.

"Well," Luke began, "We found a couple of good runs, just north of the big spring. There's a large stand of oak trees in there. The deer probably feed on the acorns during the late fall and winter when the prairie grasses dry up and get buried with snow."

"There are two real good trails," Ryan continued, "One goes from the prairie hay fields down into a low brush area along the hillside where they can bed down and catch any scent coming up from the river valley, or, coming over the hilltop from the prairie. The other trail goes from the oaks down along the low area next to the swamp where they probably bed down and have an escape route out into the thick willow brush in the swamp. We found several good scrapes along this trail."

"I think we heard them stirring around in that thick willow brush in the swamp," Luke said, "when we approached that area. All of these trails have fresh droppings, so they are very actively used."

Meanwhile," Bob said, "I explored that area at the far northern end of the farm. There's that very large washout, about a quarter mile long. Its brush filled and has some scrub-oaks out on the delta by the river. There's a very good deer run going from the prairie fields down through the washout. I found some really good scrapes along this trail. So, I'm thinking a nice buck or two."

"I think I'll just hunt along that big tamarack swamp behind the old farm buildings," Jerry said, "I saw some good signs and trails around the tamaracks, the last time I was up at the farm. Now all we have to do is put up our tree stands and wait for the season to start. We have about four days to wait."

ROBB FELDER

THE SKELETON IN THE WELL

"There should be some time to do some serious exploring of the ancient ruins before they bury them forever," Jerry said. "There are still two possible gold sites to be explored. One is in the well of the old farmhouse. The other one is in the chimney of the ancient brewery ruins. We will have to get to these before Billy and Frank do. I recommend we start this afternoon. I know the weather is crappy, but maybe Billy and Frank won't be out in it. They are probably both drunk already, celebrating their court victory."

"So, Dad," questioned Bob, "just what did happen in court this morning?"

"Well, just as I suspected, that cheese company provided some high powered lawyer to negotiate a plea deal for Billy and Frank, from a felony, down to a misdemeanor and probation. However they have been fired from their jobs as security for the cheese company property."

"Does that mean they won't be living in the old granary anymore?" Ellen asked.

"Well, they'll probably stay there for a while, I suspect, until they can find someplace else to live, or the cheese company throws them out. So meantime, we'll have to be constantly on our toes, watching out for them as we do our exploring. No telling when or where they'll show up next."

"What are we going to explore this afternoon?" Luke questioned.

"I think we'll check out the old farmhouse. There's actually not much left of it after Billy and Frank torched it back in 1986, and blamed it on Uncle Lewis."

"I understand it's just a pile of charred rubble now," Bob said.

"Yeah, we're going to have to dig down through the rubble to get to the well in the basement."

He didn't want to tell them about Lewis's skeleton in the well. He didn't want to scare them off.

"That sounds like awful dirty work to me," Brittany said, "I don't think Ellen and I would enjoy getting all filthy from a bunch of charred black wood, just to see if there's more buried treasure in the well."

"Ok then," Jerry said, "Bob, why don't you and the girls go and get your tree stands set up. The boys and I will dig into the old farmhouse."

The two groups went out to their separate missions. Bob, Ellen and Brittany went to set up their tree stands, and Jerry, Ryan and Luke to dig into the old farmhouse.

Jerry eased his new Ford, F150 truck slowly and quietly past the old granary, where under darkened skies, the lights were on in the third floor of the old granary, and that rusty old brown Chevy truck was again parked out front. Jerry pulled up behind the old farmhouse where he was obscured from view, both from the granary and the highway by the trees and the huge ancient lilac hedge that ran for about a hundred feet and for the last century separated the farmhouse and brewery from the old farmyard. The cold drizzle was still falling. The heavy dark sky made it feel like it was already late evening, although it was really only about one o'clock. It was shaping up to be a very dark and damp Halloween eve. Jerry and the boys grabbed their shovels and picks from the back of the truck and proceeded to the blackened and charred farm house. There wasn't much left above ground; part of the south wall with a single window still intact, charred black with soot stood staring down hauntingly and the blackened old brick chimney were all that were left standing. The rest of the ancient brew masters/farmhouse was nothing but blackened rubble, crumbled down into the basement.

Back in 1986 the fire was started by Frank and Billy to cover their dirty deed and start the rumor that Lewis had started the fire and then fled back to California. By the time the Otter Falls Fire Dept. had arrived, the house was totally consumed beyond hope of saving. The charred remains were never cleaned up by the cheese company, because it was considered an active crime scene of possible criminal arson. But the mystery had never been solved because Lewis was never located or heard from again and he had no next-of-kin.

They donned their gloves, rain gear and boots and Jerry led the boys around to where a stairway had led down into the basement. They began pulling apart the charred wood. Just as Jerry had suspected, the stairway was still somewhat intact, albeit, covered by charred debris and somewhat rotted from years of exposure to the elements. They began clearing away the debris and tossing it into the basement, off to the side of the old stairway, as they made their way down. At the bottom there was a small area between the end of the steps and the basement wall.

The walls were stone masonry. Like most houses built in the mid to late 1800's, the basements consisted of just one small room, most always used as a root cellar to store canned goods and keep root vegetables cool. This was because, back then, they just didn't have the availability of the powered digging machines, so the digging of those basements had to be dug by hand, by men with shovels. Because the basement walls didn't extend all the way out to the outer walls of the house, the house walls rested on separate footings.

As Jerry and the boys reached the bottom of the stairs, they could see that the old water pump and tank sat off to one side, all rusted and weathered. The water line, an old leaded pipe, that had run from the pump, through the wall into the well, was disconnected. The well itself was not in the basement, but sat outside the house, under the floor of the back porch, which was covered by a concrete slab. The access opening into the well had been cemented over, either by the cheese company, or by Frank and Billy to hide their grisly crime. They would have to chop through the patched up hole in the wall to gain access to the well.

"Is that where the gold is, Grandpa?" questioned Ryan.

"Probably not," he replied, "But we need to check it out and see what's in there."

He didn't tell them what they might find in there, because he didn't want to frighten them, and because he wasn't quite sure what they would find. He didn't know if he could believe the story told him by the likes of Frank, obviously a desperate psychopath. He had to see for himself, if the story was true. So they took turns chopping into the sealed up opening of stone masonry with their picks. Finally, after about an hour of chiseling at the wall, they had a hole large enough to squeeze through. Jerry stuck his head and shoulders through the opening and shined his flashlight down into the well. The well went down about six feet. There was no water in the well, nor was there a well pipe. That had been removed by that cheese company. There in the bottom of the well, half-buried in the sand was a skeleton.

"So, it was true," Jerry exclaimed, out loud.

"What's true?" Ryan and Luke said together.

Jerry pulled his head and shoulders back into the basement room.

"I guess I owe you guys an explanation. I haven't yet told you the story of why there's a skeleton down in the well."

"There's a skeleton in there?" the boys both said, excitedly, practically shouting, again at the same time.

"Yes, there is, and here's the story behind it. Earlier, last summer, on one of my trips up here to the old brewery, I was held at gunpoint by Billy and Frank. They said they would kill me if I didn't tell them where the gold was hidden. In the process of threatening me into telling them about the gold, Frank confessed to killing Uncle Lewis, after torturing him, trying to get him to tell them where the gold was. They dumped his body down the well and torched the house, then spread the rumor that Lewis did it and ran off to California. He hasn't been heard from since. So I now believe that's his skeleton down there."

"Wow!" Luke said, "Let us take a look."

The boys took turns peering down into the old well.

"Unbelievable," Ryan said, "I've never seen a real skeleton before. Is there also gold down there?"

"No," Jerry replied, "I'll also explain that. But first I need to go down into the well and visit Uncle Lewis."

"What?" exclaimed Luke, "Are you crazy? I think we need to call the police. This is probably a crime scene."

"Well, first give me a hand with this rope that I brought with. We need to tie loops in the rope every foot apart."

They all set about tying the loops in about six feet of the rope. Jerry tied the other end to the old water pump and lowered the looped end down into the well. Using the loops like a rope ladder, Jerry climbed slowly down into the well towards Lewis's skeleton. When he reached the bottom, he shined his flashlight at the skeleton and he could see that, just as he suspected, Lewis was still clinging to the folio that contained his 'special side deal' with the cheese company for the sale of the brewery, property and farmyard and house. Inside the folio, Jerry hoped would be a bank check for fifty thousand dollars that Lewis took to his death. He leaned over his uncle Lewis and pried Lewis's boney fingers loose from around the folio. He tucked the folio into his belt and before he began climbing back up the rope, he noticed a large hole in the middle of Lewis's forehead.

Ryan was waiting at the top and asked, "Are you alright Grandpa?"

"Yah, I'm fine, I got what I came down here for," as he brushed away any sign that he had been near the skeleton.

Ryan helped him back up through the hole in the well wall. They pulled the rope back up and untied it from the old pump.

"We may need this rope again, when we go

after the real gold, later."

Jerry then explained the story behind the folio as he went through the papers in the folio and said, "I've got to get this bank draft to the bank to see if it is still valid. And also to get it out of here in case we're accosted by Billy and Frank later."

So they loaded up their gear and headed into town, under the dark skies and the continual drizzle. Jerry went to his bank and had the bank draft verified. It was still good, in spite of being forty years old. So he deposited it into his account. As he was leaving the bank, he got a call from Bob, who said that they had Ellen's and Brittany's and his tree stands set up.

"Why don't we meet up at the McDonalds here in town? I want to discuss the rest of our day."

They all met at the McDonalds and had a late lunch, or, an early supper, they couldn't decide because it was already three o'clock. Jerry told Bob and Ellen and Brittany about finding Lewis's skeleton, and the folio with the bank draft.

"But, I thought there was gold in the well," Brittany said.

"Well, yes, and no," Jerry whispered, "There was no gold in the well that we explored so far today. That's because there's another well."

"What? Another well?" Luke said, in a whisper.

"That's correct," Jerry continued, also in a whisper, "This is a fact that Billy and Frank never found out about. Not many people know about it.

MYSTERY ON THE OTTER TAIL

Here's the story. I remember it from first-hand experience. Back in 1954, when electricity was brought into the farm and brewery, the well was actually located in the garage. It was located there originally, back when the house was built in the mid 1800's. When the Feiffers bought the house in about 1920, they built an attached garage right over the old well and pump. That was a good idea because the old pump was inside, protected from the elements and easier to prevent from freezing up, which was a common problem with those old outdoor hand pumps. So in 1954 when they wanted to install a new electric pump and indoor plumbing, they didn't want to rip up a good section of the garage floor to bury the water line, so they decided to just sink a new well out under the back porch. They removed the old hand pump, but they didn't fill in the old well. They just covered the opening with a heavy trapdoor. Typically these old wells were dug about six to eight feet deep, to be below the frost line and about four feet square. This was done to allow access to the pump cylinder, which was an enlarged section of the pipe located near the bottom of the well. This cylinder was about four or five inches in diameter and about a foot long. This cylinder had a check valve mounted in the bottom of the cylinder. Also inside the cylinder was the piston which was connected by a steel rod, up inside the pipe to the pump handle at the top of the pump. This piston also had a check valve in it. When the pump handle was pushed down, it raised the piston and water was drawn into the cylinder, opening the check valve at the bottom, closing the valve in the piston and forcing the water up and out of the pump spout. The check valve in the cylinder bottom then closed and sealed the water in the cylinder. When the pump handle was lifted up, the piston was forced down, opening the valve in the piston as it went down through the trapped water in the cylinder. When the piston was at the bottom, the cycle was ready to be repeated."

"Ok, Grandpa," Brittany said, "Thanks for the physics lesson, but what's that got to do with the gold."

"Oh, Brittany, you're such a millennial. I'm trying to teach a history lesson here, and you just want to get to the good stuff," Jerry teased.

"I was just trying to explain why there were two wells out at the old farmhouse, and I'll have to admit, I do like to digress. It's a malaise of the aged. Anyway, - - -, these old wells were very good hiding places for all sorts of things."

"Like bodies," Ryan said.

"And, - - - -," as Jerry pointed a finger at Brittany.

"Gold!" she almost shouted.

"Ok, now that I've got everyone psyched, I think we should go back out to the farmhouse and look for that second well. It's getting late, but I think we'll have time yet, before nightfall, and hopefully Billy and Frank will still be too drunk to pursue us."

They all got into the two trucks and went back out to the old farmhouse, again being careful to drive very quietly past the old granary. They pulled up again behind the burnt out old farmhouse. It was still drizzling and cold as the late afternoon grew into an early dusk under heavy dark skies.

"This sure is going to be a dismal, dreary Halloween," Luke commented.

"And very spooky," Ryan said, "we've already met the ghost and the skeleton."

"The question is, will there be a treat or a trick, for us at the bottom of the old well," Bob said.

Jerry led everyone to where the old garage once stood.

"So, where's the skeleton?" Ellen asked.

"It's in the other well."

"Can we see it?"

"Ok," Jerry said, "Ryan, why don't you show the girls the skeleton in the other well"

"Follow me," Ryan said as he led them to the other side of the basement and down the stairs.

"I don't know if I want to see a real skeleton," Brittany said, as they descended the stairs.

"Oh, com'on," Ellen said, "Don't be a chicken, this is very exciting."

Jerry, Bob and Luke stood watching and waiting at the old garage site.

"This should be good," Bob said.

As Ellen stuck her head through the opening in the wall, they all heard, "Oh, wow, very cool."

As Brittany stuck her head through the opening, they all heard a loud 'blood-curdling' scream, and Brittany came running up the stairs.

"Oh, my God, you guys, that is so gross. I've never seen a real live skeleton before."

"No, don't you mean a real 'dead' skeleton," Ellen teased her.

"Oh God, I can never un-see that. I'm going to have nightmares the rest of my life."

The evening was turning into nightfall and the drizzle had finally let up, but a heavy fog began to settle in. They all began digging through the burnt rubble until they exposed the section of the garage floor where the ancient well was. Again, there was a trapdoor in the floor, for access to the well. As Bob grabbed the steel handle, everyone stood by with their flashlights ready, trying to imagine what might be at the bottom of this well. Luke also grabbed onto the handle and they both pulled. The heavy plank trapdoor slowly creaked open. They all shined their flashlights and peered down into the musty smelling, old ancient well.

"Look, there's something down there, in the bottom," Ellen said, "Thank God, it's not another skeleton."

"It's got to be the gold," Brittany said, hopefully.

"It looks like a box of something," Ryan said.

"We've got to get down there and get it out," Luke said, "Maybe we can use that rope ladder thing, Grandpa."

Jerry ran and got the rope ladder from his truck.

Bob said, "Let's tie it over there to that section of the remaining wall."

He tied the end of the rope to a solid piece of the charred wall. Jerry climbed down into the well. He examined the boxes and found that they were old wooden beer cases. There appeared to be three of them, musty, but not too badly rotted. As he attempted to lift one of them, he found it to be very heavy. He opened the lid and shined his flashlight into the box. It was almost filled to the top, with large coins. Silver coins. When he examined one of the coins, he found that it was a silver dollar coin. The old wooden beer case was filled with silver dollar coins, hundreds, maybe thousands of them.

"How's it going down there, Dad?" Bob asked.

"Well these beer cases are really heavy. I don't think I can lift them up out of here by myself."

"Please tell me there's gold in there and not another skeleton." Brittany said.

"It's neither," Jerry said as Bob descended the rope ladder to help. Together they lifted the first one up to the trapdoor.

"Ok, you guys grab this and pull it up through

the trapdoor," Jerry said.

They did the same with the other two cases of coins, and Jerry and Bob climbed back up the rope ladder. As they crawled up out of the trapdoor, they pulled up the rope and closed the trapdoor. Luke and Ryan had opened one of the boxes.

"What's with all these old coins?" Luke asked.

"That's a good question," Jerry said. There isn't any paperwork that mentions silver dollar money."

"And why would they have kept it in the well next to the house?" Ellen asked.

"Well, I guess we'll have to make some assumptions based on what we do know about what was going on back during Prohibition. First of all, the silver dollar was a prime form of currency back then. The reason for this was mainly that people didn't trust the paper money, and they didn't much trust the banks. They wanted the 'hard' currency. They wanted silver and gold. Something they knew would hold its value. As Prohibition wore on, the price of bootleg booze kept going up, due to increased demand, as more and more people were going to the speakeasies. By the mid 1920's they were paying about a dollar for a thirty two ounce bottle of bootleg beer. So as the silver dollar became the main source of income for the August and Joe's bootleg business, it became impossible to transport hundreds of pounds of silver to the bank, or out to South Dakota to convert into gold bullion. So August just kept the silver dollars here, at home"

"So how come he didn't just spend them over the years?" asked Ryan.

"There are several reasons for that, I think. First of all, after Grandpa's bootleg operation was almost busted by the ATF, in 1926, he couldn't spend large amounts of his money. The ATF and the FBI were monitoring his bank account. Plus, he had to maintain the secrecy of the bootlegging, even after he had to shut it down. Also, remember that Grandma Annie and all of their daughters didn't know about any of the bootlegging. So he just kept the silver dollar coins hidden in the well, and he would spend small amounts of them from time to time."

"But, why were there so many of them left?" Ellen asked.

"Well, the history of the silver dollar is a sordid one. Beginning in the 1860's, during the Civil War, the US Treasury began minting the silver dollar to help pay for the war. This new silver dollar was called the 'Morgan' silver dollar. But the silver supply was limited, so the minting was rather small. However after the Civil War, as the West was being more and more settled, a very large strike of silver was discovered in Nevada. The silver strike was so large, that the US Treasury built a new mint in Carson City, Nevada to be near the source of the silver. From this mint, they turned out millions, if not billions of the silver dollars, from the 1860's through about 1902.

There were probably more silver dollars in circulation than paper dollars. By 1902 the silver dollar minting all but ceased. The huge silver mines of Nevada were petering out, and the US Treasury had enough silver dollar coins in circulation. After World War I, however they minted a fairly large number of the silver dollars called the 'peace dollar', from 1921 thru 1923. After that, they ceased minting silver dollars altogether, until the Eisenhower silver dollar in 1965. After World War I, the US Treasury recalled several hundred million of the Morgan and Peace silver dollars. They were melted down into silver bullion bars and sold on the international market to help pay for World War I. By the end of the 1930's, the 'Morgan' silver dollar was taken out of circulation, and Grandpa couldn't spend any more of them. So they just sat here in the well all those years."

"So these silver dollars are worthless," Ryan said.

"Oh, no, no, no, far from it. While you couldn't spend any of them today, keep in mind that these coins are ninety nine, point nine percent pure silver, and they weigh one ounce each. Today's price on the silver market is about twenty dollars an ounce. So, each one of these coins is worth twenty dollars."

"Wow," Brittany said, "And there are maybe thousands of these coins in these three boxes. That's as good as gold."

"Well, almost, plus some of these may be rare

collector coins, and a numismatist, or coin collector would pay hundreds, even thousands for a rare coin. The trick will be to get all of these coins sold. But for now, let's get these loaded onto the trucks and out of here before Billy and Frank show up and spoil our little Halloween party.

So each pair of them grabbed a case, together and carried them over and had just got them loaded on the trucks, and were about to get in and head for town, when out of the fog and blackness of nightfall, they heard voices coming toward them through the fog. They all stopped and froze with a knowing fright. Jerry recognized the voices right away. They all shined their flashlights through the fog in the direction of the voices, as Billy and Frank stepped out of the black fog into the light, again holding guns, of course.

"Well, well," said Billy, "trick, or treat. What have we here? Looks to me like you Feiffers have went and gotten yourselves a little Halloween treat. Get yourselves lined up against the side of that truck there. Frank, you keep your gun on them, and your flashlight. If anyone moves, shoot em."

Billy went around to the back of the truck and opened the tailgate.

"Well, lookie here, we've got boxes of gold. Good job, Feiffers. Where'd you get these? Down in the brewery?"

"No," Jerry said, "They were in the well."

"Well, I ain't never seen no boxes in that well. You lying to me again Feiffer? Cause if you are, I'm gonna shoot your ass. I don't trust a damn thing you say anymore, after last time."

"There's a second well, over there, where the old garage once stood."

"Well, I'm jus gonna walk over there and take me a look. If you're lying again, you're a dead man. Frank, keep your eye on em, they're a tricky bunch. Any of em moves, shoot em."

Billy walked over to the old garage ruins. In a minute, he came back.

"Well, I'll be damned, gold in the other well. No damn wonder we couldn't find it."

With that, Billy climbed into the back of the truck. "I'll just have a look see, at all that gold"

As he opened one of the beer cases, He just stood there momentarily, as if in shock. Then he angrily grabbed the box and tipped it over, as the coins went flying out onto the tailgate and onto the ground.

"Damn it Feiffer, What the hell is going on here?" he shouted, " Where the hell's the gold?"

"That's all we found in that well," Jerry said.

"You mean, just these worthless damn coins? Who the hell wants these?"

Nobody said a word about what Jerry had told them about the silver dollars, as Billy ranted on.

"I want my damn gold, and I won't stop till I find it. When your uncle Lewis was in prison with my stepdad, he said there was gold hidden somewhere in the old brewery, and I intend to find it."

"Wait, wait," Frank said, "You guys didn't

dig into that other well by the basement, did you?"

"Yes we did," Jerry said, "and we found Lewis's skeleton, and we have called the county sheriff. He's probably on his way out here right now."

"Ooh, no, no, no, what the hell did you go and do that for, Feiffer. Oh, damn, Billy, we've got to get the hell out of here, right now."

Billy jumped down from the truck and said, "We'll be back Feiffer, and then we're gonna find that damn gold, if it's the last thing we do. Or you're all dead, got it?"

Then the two of them disappeared into the black fog. The Feiffers all quickly picked up the spilled coins and tipped the box back up and closed the lid. They quickly got into the truck and took off for town, through the fog and blackness of the Halloween night. As they passed by the old granary, they didn't see any lights on, and the old rusty brown Chevy truck was not there anymore.

"I wonder where they went?" Ryan said.

"I don't have any idea, and I really don't care, as long as they stay gone." Jerry said.

When they got back to the motel, they put one of the coin boxes into each of their rooms and set their suitcases on top so that the cleaning crew wouldn't find that they had, possibly thousands of dollars in antique coins in their rooms.

"Wow!" Brittany said as they were carrying in the coin boxes, "That was truly the most terrifying experience of my life."

"I know," Ellen said, "those two guys are truly frightening psychopaths."

"Well, try to get some sleep," Jerry said, "We'll get together and talk about it in the morning."

They all slept fitfully, and consequently slept in late and missed the motel breakfast. They discovered that the temperature had fallen during the night, as predicted. Consequently there was a coating of ice covering everything, from the drizzle and fog freezing. The sanding trucks were out treating the streets and highways with salt. Before they left the motel, Jerry made a call to the Sheriff's Office, and reported finding Lewis's skeleton in the well at the old Feiffer farmhouse. The Sheriff looked up the old cold case, and agreed that it was probably Lewis. He said that he would send out a forensics team to re-examine the scene and remove the skeleton. The Feiffers made their way carefully up town and they all met up at the Otter Cafe for a brunch. They ordered their brunch as Jerry told them about his call to the Sheriff, and they began discussing their situation. They all agreed that while last night's encounter had been a terrifying experience, maybe with the sheriff being called in and Billy and Frank making a run for it, would give them some security for further exploration.

"Maybe, the skeleton being exposed will keep Frank and Billy away," Jerry said, "We still have four days to wait before deer hunting season opens."

MYSTERY ON THE OTTER TAIL

* * * *

As the team was discussing their possibilities, the sheriff and the forensics team along with the County Coroner arrived at the old Feiffer farmhouse. They proceeded to the basement and the Coroner began the job of extracting Lewis's skeleton from the well. They were unaware that they were being watched. Across the highway and railroad tracks, on a hilltop, in an old abandoned barn, two sets of binoculars were trained on them.

"They're pull'in Lewis's skeleton out of the well," Frank said to Billy. "Damn those Feiffers. Now they can really nail us."

"You mean, they can nail you, "Billy said, "It wasn't my idea; you shot him. You and your damn shooting everybody. Jus like you shot that whore, back in Fargo after she said you raped her. They never did find her body after we dumped it into the Red River, forty miles north of town."

"Well dammit, I thought you wanted Lewis shot. Now we.ve got to get the hell out of here."

"I know, I know, Frank," Billy said, "but how the hell can we do that? We have no money, now that we've lost our jobs at the cheese company. We've got to get back over there and find that gold. When we do, we can get the hell out of this place for good and get to California, or Mexico, or some warm place."

ROBB FELDER

RETURN TO THE BREWERY

"Well, we may as well fill up our time with some more exploring, "Bob said.

"Yes, there's still one more possibility of finding more gold," Jerry said, "There's just one more circle on the map, and it's under the old brew house, in the base of the chimney. The thing is, we're running out of time, with the cheese company threatening to bulldoze the whole place at any time."

"Well, I vote we go for it," Ryan said.

"Me too," agreed Brittany, "Maybe this time we'll get some gold. So long as they're no more skeletons."

Ellen and Luke also agreed to do more exploring, at least until deer hunting season opened. So they finished their brunch and another cup of coffee. By noon, they headed back over to their motel, to pick up their gear. The freezing drizzle had stopped, but the skies still looked dark and heavy, like it might start snowing. They took warm clothing because the temperature was still below freezing. They carefully made their way out to the old brewery ruins. The highway was ice free because of all the salting and sanding, but the long driveway into the farm and brewery was still ice covered and treacherous. The sheriff and forensic people had completed their tasks and had left. The forensic team went on into town, however, the sheriff made a stop at the old granary where he knew Billy and Frank lived. He searched the third floor room, which was nothing more than a grain bin. He found what he was looking for and left, and headed back into Otter Falls. Jerry assumed they would have the place to themselves, with Billy and Frank gone. They pulled up in front of the ancient brewery ruins and donned their backpacks and made their way around to the back side of what was left of the old bottling plant. Jerry led the way into the basement and back into the small room with the old rotted beer vat.

"This is starting to look kinda creepy," Brittany said, "You sure there's no skeletons in here?"

"I make no promises," Jerry said, "Just follow me."

He led the way to the back corner of the room, to the tunnel.

"Wow," exclaimed Ellen, "A tunnel. This is way cool."

They all crawled through the tunnel and into the next room, under the old brew house and Jerry lit an old lantern. The crew all gathered around the old steel hops strainer as Jerry explained its function. He went on to tell them about the last time he and David and Zachary and Colby were there, and the discovery of the beer case full of paper money, hidden in the steel tank.

"Wow," Ryan said, "This old brewery is just full of money."

"Well, it does seems like your great, great grandfather, August, had a very profitable bootlegging operation, a hundred years ago," Jerry said, "Unfortunately for them, back then they couldn't spend a lot of it because it was all illegal, but lucky for us."

"Ok, what do you think we'll find today?" Luke said, "will it be more coins, or paper money, or gold this time?'

"Is the gold in this room?" Ryan asked, "Or do we have to bust through a wall again?"

"Well, yes, and no," Jerry replied, "We have to find the access to the old chimney, which is just outside this room. The bad news is, the access is under that old crumbled down stairs."

He pointed to a huge pile of rubble on one side of the room.

"That used to be the stairway coming down from the main floor. But, when they tore down the upper floors, the rubble just came crashing down through the stairway opening and crushed down the steps and filled the opening from floor to ceiling with broken bricks and debris. We're going to have to dig through that pile of rubble to get at the access door to the chimney."

"Well, it looks like if we want the gold, we're

going to have to work for it," Bob said.

"We may as well get to work then," Luke said.

"Ok, here's a plan," Jerry said, "let's form two teams. One team will throw the bricks and debris off to the right side. The other team will toss to the left. We can hand off the old bricks to one another. Be careful though, of falling debris as we dig further into the pile."

They all opened their backpacks and pulled out gloves, picks and shovels. Some of the rubble contained large chunks of brick wall that had to be chopped and broken apart, before being able to move it to the new rubble piles. They worked at a pretty good pace for about an hour, and put a fairly large dent in the pile. So they took a little break and had an energy bar and some water.

"Boy, this would go a lot faster, if we had a bobcat down here," Ryan said.

"I know," Ellen said, "but we sure are getting a good workout, digging all these bricks out."

The crews went back to work, chipping and picking at the large chunks of wall and tossing the debris onto the new piles. After another hour, they began to see daylight coming through the stairwell opening in the floor above. They noticed that it was already starting to get dark, with the heavy, overcast cloud cover. They continued working feverishly for another hour, and had a hole in the rubble pile large enough to crawl out through. They looked up through the opening and saw a starry sky.

Bob said, "It looks like its totally dark out. It's getting late. I think it's time to knock off for today."

"I agree," Brittany said, "I sure could use a rest, I'm totally exhausted. I sure hope we're getting closer to the gold."

"I know", Ellen said, "We've worked our butts off today, digging out all that old brick rubble."

"Are we even getting close to the back wall where the chimney is?" Ryan asked.

"Yah," Jerry replied, "I think another couple hours of digging should do it. But that's for tomorrow. Let's grab our gear and head back to town and get some dinner and a good night's sleep."

They all grabbed their packs and climbed up the rubble pile and out through the opening and headed for the trucks.

ROBB FELDER

MYSTERY ON THE OTTER TAIL

THE LAST HURRAH

Meanwhile, across the highway and the railroad tracks, on the hilltop, in the old barn, the two recluses were just getting up after sleeping most of the day. They crawled out from under the pile of old hay. They had been sleeping off a drunk from the night before.

"C'mon, Frank, get yer lazy butt up," Billy said, "it's time to go and git our gold."

"Has that sheriff left yet? And those damn Feiffers?"

"Yah, they're just now leav'in', I can see their truck lights jus pull'in' out."

"Ok, let's git back over to the granary and git us some food, I'm starv'in'."

They made their way down the hill and across the highway and railroad tracks, just after the Feiffer's trucks passed by on their way into town. They walked in the dark up the driveway to their home in the old granary and climbed the stairs to the third floor.

"Wait," Billy said, "Before we can light the lantern, we got to cover these here windows. So's nobody knows we're back in here."

They took the blankets off of their beds and

tacked them up on the windows, and then lit the old kerosene lantern. Frank lit the old rusty propane stove and opened a couple of cans of soup and dumped them into an old sauce pan. They opened up a half loaf of the old stale bread and ate the soup from bowls that had not been washed for weeks because there wasn't any water available, and they could no longer afford to buy water, because they choose to buy booze instead. After they had eaten their supper of soup and the dried out bread, Billy said, "Well, let's wash that down with some good brew."

He picked up a six pack of Linnies and opened it and tossed one to Frank. The beer was fairly warm because there was no refrigerator, of course, because there was no electricity. They chugged their beers and popped open another, as they talked about how great life was going to be when they got their gold.

"When we lay our hands on that gold," Billy said, "we can get the heck out of this crappy place."

"We can get us a new pickup truck and hightail it for Mexico," Frank said, "I heard they got some really hot wimmin down there."

After that one, they popped open another. They began talking about the Feiffers and how they were screwing up their plans and their lives.

"Those damn Feiffers," Frank said, as he opened another six-pack, and tossed another beer to Billy, "we should'da jus shot em all when we had the chance."

"You and your damn shoot'in people," Billy said, "that's why we're in this jam in the first place. Dammit, I told you not to shoot Lewis back then, by that well. You have to learn how to use people instead of always shooting em."

They argued about it some more as they finished that beer and opened another. As they were downing that one, they were entering the, 'sentimental' phase of their drunk.

"You remember, Frank, the shit we were in, back when we wuz in the Army, over in Nam. Boy, that wuz some hell-hole of a place. Remember how we used to 'smoke' them gooks out of their tunnels. We'd toss in a bunch of tear-gas grenades and when they came running out, we'd mow em down with our 'AK's. Poor bastards, couldn't see a damn thing from the tear gas in their eyes. We'd just kill and kill and kill, till there was a pile of em jus' outside their tunnel hole."

"Ya," frank said, "We'd kill em all day, then when we got R and R in Saigon, we'd party with their wimmin all night."

* * * *

These were two desperately damaged war veterans. One was repulsed by the bloody massacre and carnage of war. The other became addicted to it.

ROBB FELDER

* * * *

"We sure had it good, though," Frank said, "Back when we wuz livin' in Fargo, after the war. We wuz makin' some good money back then too. drivin' dump truck for the highway department. We had us a real nice townhouse, and had us some real hot wimmin."

Yah," Billy said, "But then I had to go and meet up with that blonde 'she-devil'. Boy, oh boy, did she take us for a ride. Everything was goin so great, but then she wanted to move in with us and when we was drinkin' she would want to party all night long and take turns with each of us."

"I, know, sometimes, when she wuz good and drunk she would keep both of us up all night.

"But then the wheels started com'in off our sweet setup. She got busted for pass'in a bad check. When we went to court with her and paid for her lawyer, she claimed she wuz pregnant by one of us and wanted to use the lawyer that we paid for, to sue us both for paternity. The court awarded her our townhouse, and she kicked us both out."

"That's when we really started drink'in heavy and got DWI's and lost our jobs driv'in trucks. Later we learned she never wuz pregnant."

"That's when you had to go and shoot her, Frank. We dumped her body in the Red River, bout forty miles north of Fargo. That's when we moved back here to Otter Falls. My uncle Fred got us the jobs work'in security for the cheese company."

After two more beers each, Billy said, "Ok, time to take this to the next level."

"Here's to our gold," they both toasted.

They downed it, and Billy poured another. After about six more beers, they entered the 'remorse' stage, or 'self-condemnation' phase of their drunk.

"Ya know," Billy said, "After all those crappy wimmin in Fargo, I finally found me a good one when we got back here to Otter Falls. I really fell in love with Ruth Ann. We had some really good years together. Heck, we even got married and had us two kids together."

"Well, you're darn lucky, Billy ol' Buddy. I've had me some real good wimmin since we got back here, But I ain't never married one of em. An, I ain't got no kids that I know of. I guess I ain't really got no kin of any kind. Jus' you Billy, ol' Buddy."

Billy continued, "But then I screwed it all up. She threw me out. Shee - - said I drunk too mush, an dat wus bad fer the kii - -ids," Billy said as he began slurring his words, "Sheee - -saaiid I coudin effen seee myii kidds tiiill eyee sooburrd ouup. Shhee – saiid eyee wuus nuttuun but a gall damnn dee-rrunk. Eyee em a gall damn grunnk, ain't eyee, Fur-enuk?"

"Ya, Billyee, ya arree, annn sooo - - em eyee."

Then came the 'fighting', or 'confrontational

stage.

"Welll, don- -n U cal-ll me no drr-ouunk, ya damnn murrder-er-rr."

"Donn' caa-ll mee no murrder-err, or I' - -lll keell ya, ya dammnn drr- -ounk."

With those words, the two got up and squared off with one another. They ran at each other, their arms flailing, mostly in the air. They locked up arms together in a sort of hug. They stayed that way for about a minute.

Frank said, "Screw you Billy, yur my best friend."

Billy said, "Screw you Frank, I love you, man."

And then came the 'unconscious' stage, or for some,- - - - -'the blackout'.

With that, they both toppled over onto Frank's mattress on the floor. Dead drunk. Frank was out for the night. Billy however, was not. After about five minutes, he untangled himself from Frank and slowly tried to pull himself up, using the chair for support. He just stood there swaying, holding on to the chair.

After about a minute, he looked down at his buddy, and said, "Frank,- - Frank".

Another minute went by and he said again, "Frank,- - Frank, ya damn drunk."

Another minute and he said, "Frank,- - Frank, I think I just pissed my pants."

After another minute, he turned and quickly grabbed the lantern off the table and headed to the stairs. He yelled over his shoulder, "Frank, I don't feel so good."

Billy made his way hurriedly down the stairs and out around the back to the old outhouse. He barely made it and stuck his head in the hole and vomited his guts out. Suddenly he stood up and dropped his pants and sat down and relieved himself. When finished, he pulled up his pants without wiping, because there was no paper.

He grabbed the lantern and stepped out of the outhouse and said to absolutely no one, "I'm goin to get my gold now, and if you ain't commin, Frank, then da hell whit ya, I'll get it all."

He made his way down the path, swaying and stumbling as he went, to the old brewery ruins. The night was black dark, as heavy clouds hung overhead. The temperature was dropping and a light snow was falling. Billy staggered down the path with his lantern and did not feel cold at all, even with just a light shirt on. He made his way down into the collapsed bottling plant and crawled through the tunnel into the brew house basement. He held the lantern up high to see all around the room and saw the two large piles of rubble.

He set the lantern down and walked over between the piles and kicked a few small pieces of the debris and said aloud, again to no one, "Dammit Frank, those darn Feiffers have got our gold."

He then turned around and walked over to the tunnel and crawled through it, totally unaware, that he had left his lantern behind. He slowly made his way back, stumbling along the path. As he was staggering through a wooded area along the path, he tripped on a tree root that had grown across the path. He went down, face first into the pathway. His nose and face were badly skinned up, but he didn't feel a thing. He just laid there for about twenty minutes. The snow was beginning to cover him. Finally, miraculously, he stirred and his body gave a few twitches. He slowly pushed himself up into a kneeling position and crawled over to a small tree near the path and slowly pulled himself up on his feet again, wobbling, he clung to the tree. He attempted to walk, but began to convulse and vomit. There was nothing more in his stomach, but he continued to convulse and wretch in what is commonly known as the 'dry heaves', as he staggered along the path back to the old granary and climbed the stairs to the third floor. He collapsed onto his mattress.

Just before he fell into a deep drunken, 'black-out' sleep, he muttered, "Frank, Frank."

Sadly, the next morning he would not remember any of this.

KIDNAPPED

THE END GAME

The Feiffer troop started waking up, slowly, and later than they really wanted too. Yesterday's workout in the brew house basement was having an effect on their wakeup. There was that, - - -, and also the effect of the first look outside. Snow was coming down steadily, with about four inches on the ground already. In northern Minnesota, and probably all across the northern tier of the US, and probably the earth, there's that period of, 'denial-acceptance', as northern humans struggle with the acceptance part of it. The 'it', being the subconscious knowledge that we are all, now, being cast into a new world of ice and snow for the next six months. A world in which we are now confined, as in a sentence, to our, 'inside' world. An inside world of our own creation, forbidden and banished from the beautiful, natural world, which has now become, for the most part, uninhabitable and forbidding.

They trickled down into the breakfast room of the motel, at the end of the serving hours. The selections were limited, but what they all really craved was that magic elixir called coffee. which pushes one over a definite line in the conscious between groggy and alert. It's always amazing how rapidly the caffeine can wake a person up. In a few minutes, they all had their appetites back in working order and were wolfing down the remnants of the available breakfast items. While they were eating, they were discussing yesterday's struggles and todays possibilities. After they had all eaten, they were relaxing and enjoying their second and third cups.

Bob finally said to Jerry, "What's the plan for today boss? The same, I suspect," as he answered his own question.

"Yah, that's correct," Jerry said, "We've got to get to that gold and get it out of there. We've got pressing time issues to deal with. One is, of course, that damn Billy and his half-crazy side kick, Frank, who is probably the murderer of Uncle Lewis."

"Those two terrify us so bad," Ellen said, also speaking for Brittany. "Are you sure we have to go."

"I kind of think those two are really scared off after we called the sheriff," Jerry said.

"Well, we sure could use your help," Bob said, "the more help we have, the sooner we can get to the gold."

That convinced Brittany, who said, hesitatingly, "Well, okay, if we can get the gold and get out of there before they show up again."

"So, Grandpa," Ryan said, "what was that other time thing we have to pay attention to?"

"Well, the cheese company, which still owns the ancient brewery, is threatening to bulldoze the whole place level, because of all the troubles with the murder and everything, and they want to get it done before winter. They couldn't do it before this because it was a crime scene. But now with Lewis's skeleton removed, it's no longer a crime scene."

With their late start and long discussions, it was now noon. so they watched the noon hour news, and mostly the weather. The weather person said that the snow would end soon, and the sun would melt most of the snow in the afternoon. But more snow would be coming in tonight.

"Well, that doesn't give us a lot of time. We better get to work," Jerry said.

They all agreed, and went to get their gear and themselves loaded into the trucks. They arrived at the ancient ruins and started to crawl back down into the opening they had made in the stairwell rubble when Jerry got a call from the sheriff. The sheriff said he wanted to get together and talk about the autopsy on Lewis's skeleton.

"Okay," Jerry said come on out, we're in the basement of the old brew house."

"Well, I also wanted to warn you. The cheese company is sending out a crew and equipment to bury the place this afternoon. They asked me to get everybody out. So you guys don't have much time to get your excavating done, to find whatever you're looking for. Gold, you said, or whatever."

They ended the call and Jerry quickly crawled down into the basement.

"What was that call about?" Bob asked.

"That was the sheriff, he said he'll be out later to talk about Lewis's autopsy. He also said the cheese company is sending out a crew and equipment to bury this place for good. We've got to go like crazy to get that gold out of here, before they get here."

The crew went to work, same as yesterday, digging out the mountain of the bricks and rubble and tossing it to either side, getting ever closer to the back wall where the chimney base was, and the gold.

* * * * *

In the old granary, third floor, there were actually, signs of life, but it was a cold life. Frank was waking up and he was freezing, still lying there, where he had collapsed last night. He had slept all night and well into the day, without any covers, because they had used the blankets to cover the windows. He slowly rolled over, off his mattress and got to his feet. As he did so, his head throbbed like a hundred hammers beating on it. His mouth was so dry that it felt like his tongue was stuck to the roof of his mouth and was covered in wallpaper paste. His throat was burning and as dry as desert sand, and was screaming for water.

MYSTERY ON THE OTTER TAIL

"This place is fricken' freezing," He said to no one but himself.

Billy was still out cold. Frank went over to one of the windows and ripped down one of the blankets and wrapped himself up in it. He also pulled down the other blanket, and threw it over his sleeping buddy, Billy.

"There ya damn fool drunk, before ya freeze ta death."

The afternoon sun came blazing in, glaring off the new fallen snow, burning his eyeballs like hot soapy water. Outside, the temperature was already above freezing and some of the snow was melting off the roof. But little comfort inside, where there was no heat source of any kind. His teeth were chattering and his fingers were numb from the cold. He tried dancing around and stomping his feet to get his blood flowing in them again.

He was beginning to feel the need for a drink again, and he began having the shakes, as his body was screaming for some kind of liquid, any liquid, But first he had to pee, desperately. He practically ran down the stairs, and peed right outside the door of the granary. But then he needed the outhouse. There he relieved himself, but again, - -, no paper. He returned to the third floor. Now he was trembling desperately for that first beer of the morning. He rummaged around in all the debris and garbage and finally found a beer, an actual full one, after sucking the last few drops from several of last night's empties. He popped the top, and gave a huge sigh, - - -, a-h-h-h, - - -, that first swallow on a parched throat. He guzzled several more swallows, but then suddenly realized he had to save some for his friend Billy. He knew, of course, that Billy would be going through the same process that he had just gone through to satisfy his cravings and get his body functioning again. His shakes began to slowly subside as the alcohol slowly flowed into his blood stream and up to his brain, releasing the pent-up endorphins and quieting the raging addictive desperation for more of the same.

Frank pulled a chair out from the table to sit down. The scraping of the chair on the floor woke Billy. He grabbed at the blanket that Frank had tossed over him, and rolled over wrapping it tightly around him.

"Damn, it's cold in here," he said.

"Com'on, you've got to get up, Billy. We got to go get us that gold today."

"Screw the gold, dammit, I'm freez'in."

"Come on Billy. We got to get us that gold. There ain't nuth'in in this place to eat anymore. I'm starv'in, and we're both freez'in. We got to get us some winter clothes and some food."

"Awh, to heck wit all that. Lee'me alone dammit, I jus wanna sleep some more."

"Billy, come on, we gotta get goin. It's probably afternoon already."

The only reply Frank got was Billy snoring. Frank didn't know what to do. He knew Billy was a real bastard to get going in the morning. He just sat there, staring at Billy for several minutes. Suddenly Billy sat bolt-upright.

"I gotta pee," he said.

Apparently the warmth of the blanket started his body functioning again. He rolled over again, off the mattress onto the floor, still wrapped in the blanket. He reached out a hand, and Frank helped pull him to his feet. Still wrapped in his blanket like Frank was, he bee-lined for the stairs and to the outhouse. While he was gone, Frank lit the camp stove and found a few slices of the stale bread, left from last night. He stuck a fork into it and toasted it over the flame. Now he needed a beverage, He took the soup kettle and went down and filled it with snow and put it on the stove to melt.

Billy came back up, with a bad case of the shakes. Frank gave him the half can of beer and in a few minutes his shakes subsided.

"I made breakfast for you," Frank said.

They each had a couple of slices of the toasted stale bread and drank some of the melted snow water. After their 'brunch', they began discussing their strategy for getting the gold.

"Okay, here's how I see's it," Billy said, "Dem Feiffers should just about have that gold dug up what's in the old brew house. That's what it showed on that old map I stole from them at that river camp last spring. There's one of them strange circles right there in the brew house basement. I think it's buried under that ol' beer vat that kid wuz hiding in, that time last spring. Here's what we'll do. We'll wait til jus about dark. I'll slip in through that tunnel from the ol' bottling plant where we found that beer case full of worthless money. You come in through that other short tunnel from the other cellar. That way, we'll have them surrounded. If they have the gold dug up already, we'll jus grab the gold and high-tail it outta there. We'll get the keys to one of them trucks, then tie em all up. By the time they git loose, we'll be in Iowa already. We'll git some money off'n em for gas money. By morn'in, we could be in N'orleans. I've got a buddy down there, could help sell all the gold, then we'll all head for Mexico. I hear them Mexican wimmin is really hot."

"So what if the gold ain't dug up yet?"

"Well, that's where you come in. Frank. If they're still digg'in and ain't dug up the gold yet, you will take them young Feiffers as hostages. We'll first tie em up good, cause they're a tricky bunch, so watch em. You'll take em at gunpoint back over here and lock em in that hog barn basement where they used to make the bootleg, and keep them there till them older Feiffers dig up the gold. I'll stay back and hold a gun on em till they git the gold. When you git back, we high-tail it jus like the first plan, and we'll call them from N'orleans and tell them where their kids is hid."

"Why don't we jus' kill the whole damn bunch once we git our gold?"

MYSTERY ON THE OTTER TAIL

"Dammit Frank, there ya go again with the kill'in all the time. Yer start'in ta scare me. Don't go kill'in nobody unless ya have ta. Ya know, they can still come git ya in Mexico."

"Alright, alright, dammit I'll try to hold it in check. Jes' hope nobody don't trip my trigger an tick me off. I'm runn'in on a real short fuse here. I want that damn gold as much as you do,"

"Ok, ok, so let's git our guns and get ready to go."

Frank went over to a small cabinet and opened it, He handed Billy his gun, and pulled out an old Army 45 caliber, and a box of old shells.

"Where the heck did you git that from?"

"Well hell, Billy, I've had this since we was in Nam. I've jus' been sav'in' it for a special occasion. And this is gonna be pretty damn special today, gett'in' that gold."

They waited around until sundown and took a short nap while waiting, and woke just as it was getting dark out.

"Ok then," Billy said, "Let's git the heck goin"

They grabbed their guns and several hanks of the old farm rope and headed for the old brewery.

* * * *

Jerry and his crew worked frantically for an hour, then needed a break.

"We're making great progress," he said, "We've got most of the back wall cleared away. Another hour, and we should start to see that clean-out door in the chimney."

Just then they heard the sound of heavy equipment moving around above, outside. Bob climbed up the rubble pile and looked out the opening.

"It looks like they're working on covering up the old farmhouse. It won't be long and they will want to bury the whole brewery. We've got to get that gold out as quickly as possible. Also it's quite foggy out there again, and it's clouding up, and the temperature is dropping like it could start snowing again, just like they predicted."

They all went back to work, tossing bricks and debris like crazy. After about a half hour, they could see the top of the steel clean-out door at the base of the chimney. Another twenty minutes and Jerry could open the door. They all held their breath as he lifted the ancient latch and the rusty old door creaked slowly open. But there was dismay and disappointment as they saw that the chamber behind the door was filled with bricks and rubble. They should have realized that when the large chimney was knocked down, many of the bricks and mortar fell down inside the chimney. They had no choice but to work frantically and get the chamber cleared out. They were encouraged to find that the chamber was not full to the ceiling. In short order, they had most of the debris cleared out. Just then, they heard a voice coming from the mouth of the old tunnel. There stood Billy, with a gun in his hand and a loop of the rope.

"Well, well, well, sorry I'm late to the party. Or, am I right on time?"

Everybody stopped what they were doing and put their hands in the air.

"Arr-right, dammit, where's dat gold, Feiffer?"

"We haven't found any gold yet Buchanen."

"Are you jus' lying to me again, Feiffer?"

Just then Frank arrived from the other tunnel.

"We got you surrounded," He said, "Ya better give up dat gold, or somebody's go'in ta die tonight."

"Do you see any gold?" Jerry said.

"So, yer still d'gin fer it?"

"Yeah, that's correct."

"Well here's what we're gonna do, "Frank said, "I'm taken all yer young people here, hostage tonight. Keep yer gun on 'em, Billy, whilst I git 'em tied up."

Frank gave his gun to Billy and proceeded to tie up the four young people. He tied their wrists behind their backs and tied them each together in one line.

"Ok, here's the deal, Feiffer," Frank said, "I'm takin these here kids off somewhere. I won't kill them just yet, unless they try to escape. When I get back, you're goin' ta finish digg'in' fer the gold. If there's gold, you get yer kids back, after we get outta here with it. If no gold, - - - dead kids, ya got it."

Billy picked up one of the lanterns to hand to Frank.

"Say, this looks jus like our lantern," he said, "How the heck it get over here. You damn Feiffers been stealing from us?"

Frank got his gun back from Billy and with Ellen, Brittany, Luke and Ryan, left through the tunnel, single-file, all four of them tied up and tied together in a line. They disappeared into the fog outside.

After they left, Billy said, "So, you two, get back to work digg'in' for that gold. When Frank gets back, we want to be leav'in' with it, or, there'll be dead kids."

* * * *

Frank and his line of captives made their way along the pathway to the old barnyard. They stumbled along, mostly, quietly. The snow was again falling and covering the ground.

There was no sound, aside from the expected, "Where are you taking us?" And the expected reply by Frank, "None of yer damn business. You'll see soon enough."

Further down the trail, Ellen asked, "Are you going to kill us?"

"That remains to be seen. Jus keep walk'in

MYSTERY ON THE OTTER TAIL

and shut the hell up."

In the distance they could hear the grinding clatter of a bulldozer just finishing filling in and burying the old farmhouse, - - -. and it's wells.

Frank had no thoughts about what had happened in that farmhouse, - - -, in the well. He was, apparently a complete psychopath, who felt completely justified in what he had done. He led them around to the back of the old granary and over to the back of what once was the old slop kitchen. There, next to the old crumbled down chimney was the hole, which Jerry, David, Zachary and Colby had crawled out of and buried last spring. Later, Billy and Frank had dug it open again to see if there was any gold down in the old brew chamber.

"Ok, kids, down ya go, into the hole."

They all climbed and stumbled and slid down into the hole into the tunnel. He followed them down.

"Ok, now get on through that door into that next room. That is where yur grandpappy made his bootleg brew, what got us all this gold that we're after. I hear it's haunted by his ghost."

They all stumbled over the rubble and into the underground brew house. Brittany, Ellen, Luke and Ryan were pushed into the basement room, still all tied up and tied together. Frank followed them in and set the lantern down.

"I'm leav'in you this lantern out of the goodness of my heart," He then snickered and said,

"I have no doubt you'll have yourselves untied in no time. If me and Billy get our gold, you'll be out in a day or so. If no gold, your stay will just be like, - - -, forever."

He went up to Ellen and Brittany from behind and stroked Ellen's hair.

"My, my, ain't you just a pretty little woman, jus my type, nice and slim and tall, and real nice figure." as he ran his hands over her hair again and down her neck, "when I get back, I'm gonna really get to know ya.. and you blondie," he said, as he moved over to Brittany, and grabbed her from behind, running his hands up and down her. "What a nice body and a mighty pretty face too. I'd do ya both right now if I wern't in a hurry. I'm on my way back to that other brew house to get me my gold, but when I get it, I'm com'in back and get. ta know ya better. Heh, heh, heh," He chuckled to no one but himself. "Unless, no gold, then I'll have ta come back and kill ya. But I'll get ta know ya first, then kill ya all.

"You filthy bastard," Ryan yelled, "Don't you touch my cousins."

"An jus what the hell ya think you'll do about it. You'll be tied up jus like now. You'll jus git ta watch. If I don't kill ya first."

With that, Frank swung his 45 and cracked Ryan on the side of his head and knocked him down to the floor, as he turned and headed to the door.

"I'll be back, an you gals better be ready cuz I'll be getten ta know all ya real, real well."

With that he blew them a kiss and slammed the door, and piled a huge pile of rocks and rubble against it. He climbed back up out of the tunnel hole and was gone. On his way back to the brewery, he took his 45 and fired it twice into the air.

"There, that should let them damn Feiffers know we mean business," he said aloud to no one.

* * * *

The next thing the kids heard was the sound of big rocks and other rubble being thrown against the outside of the door. When there was no more sound from the outside of the door, the four finally dared speak again.

"Are you alright, Ryan?" Ellen said.

"Yeah, I think I'm okay, aside from a headache," He said, as he got up.

His ear was bleeding, and blood was trickling down his neck, but seemed to subside when he stood up. They all got to work getting each other untied. Finally, that was accomplished.

"That guy is such a perverted monster," Ellen said, "I've never been so terrified in my life. What are we going to do? We've got to get out of here before that creep comes back."

"I know, "Brittany said, "If he comes and finds us here, we're as good as dead. But, thank you Ryan, for standing up to him for us. That was really brave of you."

They all tried their cell phones, but no luck,

no reception down in this dungeon-like room, with its foot thick walls and ceiling.

"Well, let's all go to work and figure out a way out of here," Luke said.

They first tried pushing on the door, but there were too many rocks and brick debris piled against it to even budge it. They tried the other door, but it was locked from the outside.

"It looks like we're doomed," Brittany said despairingly, almost in tears, as they went over to a corner and sat down on the empty grain sacks.

They all just sat there for a very long time. After a while, just like the Feiffers of last spring, they all thought they were hearing voices. It was August and Joe, discussing the brew they were working on.

August was saying, "This mash is going to make a good batch, but according to the reading on the hygrometer, we still need to beef up our sucrose level by adding more corn to the mash, in the next batch."

"Yah." Joe was saying, "They keep wanting a higher ABV."

Suddenly Ryan stood up and shook his head. "Is anybody else hearing voices?'

"I think, I heard them too," Ellen said.

"I heard them too," Brittany said. "That's spooky. I think this place is haunted."

"Wait," Luke said, "look what I found," as he went over and picked up the steel bar that had been used before as a crow bar.

"What's that going to do for us?" Ellen said

despairingly, "We're surrounded by solid concrete."

"Ok," Luke started to explain, as he walked over to the blocked tunnel door, "This door opens outward into the tunnel. So, that means that the door jams are here on our side of the door. If we can just pry these jams off, maybe we can force the door to open into the room."

"What a great idea," Ryan said, "Sounds like it should work. Let's get to work."

Luke took the pry bar, which had a sharp edge on one end and forced it under the door jam and pried. The jam began to give way, but broke into pieces because it was so brittle with age. By moving the bar along the jam, he got it to crumble, piece by piece. It took a while, but Luke and Ryan took turns at it until they had it all removed. The door didn't move, by itself, however. They had to use the pry bar on the door itself to begin to get it to budge, because the hinges were holding it in the closed position. It took all four of them to pry on the bar and pull inward on the door. Slowly it began to loosen the hinges and open, then start to pull the hinges out of the door frame. They kept pulling, and now the rock pile on the outside of the door began to work in their favor. The weight of the rocks and their pulling suddenly broke the hinges free. The door gave way, and the door and rock pile came crashing into the room, as the four of them jumped out of the way.

They all gave out a loud cheer as the cold

night air streamed into the room.

* * * *

Jerry, Bob and Billy all thought they heard a voice from the floor above, by the stairwell opening.

"Jerry Feiffer, is that you down there?" it was the sheriff.

"Yes, we're down here," Jerry replied, "Come on down, but be careful, he's got a gun on us."

The sheriff got his gun out and proceeded to climb down through the hole and down the rubble pile. He stumbled, half-way down and went sliding on the loose rubble, and ended up lying right at the feet of Billy, who grabbed the sheriff's gun.

"Surprise, you're called out sliding into second base. Now git up and stand over there with them other two losers. They already found me one of my gold bars. When Frank gits back, they're gonna dig up the rest, and we're gonna high-tail it outta here. Meantime, Feiffer, why don' ya jus toss me the keys to yer truck."

Jerry hesitated, and said, "I heard some shots fired out there, Billy. If that damn Frank shot any of the kids, you aren't getting my keys, and you'll never get the rest of the gold."

So Billy said, "Com'on Feiffer, don' make me shoot the sheriff here. And I told Frank not to go shoot'in dem kids yet."

So Jerry tossed over the keys. Just then Frank came out of the tunnel and saw the sheriff standing there.

"What the hell is go'in on here?" he said. Can I jus shoot this damn sheriff?"

"No," Billy shouted, "I've got him covered."

"Well, okay, for now, but we don't have time to screw around wit no damn cops. So where the hell's our gold?" he demanded. "Let's have it before I start shootin."

Jerry went over to the chimney clean-out door and pulled out a gold bar and dropped it at Franks feet.

"Here's your damn gold, now take it and get the hell out of here. I just want to know what you did with my kids."

"We'll tell ya after we're outta here, free and clear," Frank said, as he picked up the gold bar and said to Billy, 'okay, let's get the hell outta here, we got our gold."

"Wait, wait, wait, there's got ta be more gold in there."

"No, Jerry said, "Come see for yourself."

He didn't let Billy know, that just like the other chimney at the old hog slop kitchen , the rest of the gold was buried beneath the floor of the chimney base. Billy came over and looked inside. He saw that the chimney base was cleared out right to the floor of the base.

"Well, I'll be damned, he said, as he turned

and said to Frank, "Ok, let's get the hell outta here."

Frank had already run to the short tunnel and crawled through with his gold bar. Billy followed. But while he had been looking in the chimney base, the sheriff had bent down and pulled a small .38 out of his ankle holster. As Billy entered the short tunnel, the sheriff fired and hit Billy in the side, but lucky for Billy, lower down and not fatal. Billy fell out of the other end of the tunnel, but got up again and ran off to the right, to the cellar that had the opening and a way out. Frank, however, became confused and headed to the left cellar with no exit.

He yelled to Billy, "This way buddy, you awright?"

"Ya, I'm okay Billy yelled, "Com'on, this way out."

Frank was still confused and yelled back, "No, Billy, this way."

They could hear, now, the sound of the bulldozer working above, pushing down the walls of the old malt kiln building.

Frank suddenly realized he was wrong. But it was too late, he had gone into the dead-end cellar, as the sheriff and Bob and Jerry came crawling through the short tunnel. Billy, meanwhile, scrambled up out of the other cellar and made for Jerry's truck. The sheriff realized the situation, he had Frank trapped.

He yelled into the cellar, "You're under arrest, Frank, for the murder of Lewis Feiffer. I found your murder weapon up in your granary room. That gun was registered to you when you started as a security guard, along with Billy. The bullet in Lewis's skeleton matches your gun."

"No, no," Frank yelled back, "I ain't never killed nobody. It musta been Billy. I'm comm'in out, but you ain't takin me in."

With that, he stepped out from behind the pillar at the far end of the cellar, near the old malt kiln building. He had the gold bar tucked under his left arm, and his .45 army pistol in his right.

Frank couldn't clearly see over to where the sheriff and the Feiffers stood in the semi-darkness of the cellar room. Just then he saw, off to his left, three shadowy figures standing there; that were not the sheriff and the Feiffers. The ghostly figures seemed to be motioning to him. He became confused by what he was seeing. Were they trying to show him a way out? He blinked several times and they became more clearly defined. They were dressed in old-time clothing. Were they August, Joe and Lewis? He panicked and began firing off the huge .45 rounds. After he had fired off about five rounds, but didn't hit anyone, of course, he started to realize, albeit too late what he had done. The shock waves from the large caliber weapon suddenly loosened up the ancient deteriorated concrete pillar next to him. The pillar collapsed, and the floor above him collapsed on top of him. He went down under it, still clinging to his gold ingot. His screams were drowned out by the roar of the collapsing concrete all around him, as the walls from the old malt kiln building also crumbled into the cellar on top of him. The bulldozer operator was oblivious to what had just happened down below. He just kept pushing the rubble from the collapsed malt kiln down into the cellar. Franks body, and his gold ingot were soon covered forever, by hundreds of tons of debris.

The sheriff and the two Feiffers just stood there for several minutes in shock and awe at what had just happened. As the clouds of dust from the collapse and the bulldozing threatened to engulf them, they quickly turned and ran into the other cellar and up and out of the ancient ruins, as the bulldozer ultimately buried the entire ancient brewery ruins under thousands of tons of dirt and debris. Whatever gold was left in the base of the chimney was also buried by about fifteen feet of the rubble. There was some proof that there were three more of the gold ingots from 1925, left in the chimney base according to August's documentation. Probably below the floor of the chimney base, in a beer keg, just like in that other chimney on the farm.

The fourth gold ingot that Frank had clung to all the way into the hereafter, along with Frank would remain buried forever. Moreover, any possibility of ever finding the location of the chimney base would be nearly impossible, because all of the floors and all the walls were collapsed into the basements and covered by many feet thickness of the dirt and debris.

MYSTERY ON THE OTTER TAIL

So the mysteries of the old brewery would continue. Some mysteries were now solved, but the mystery of the last of the gold bars would go on. Maybe, as August Feiffer had said, over one hundred years ago, "Maybe some future generation of Feiffers would dig up the ruins of the ancient brewery and discover the four gold bars and become very, very rich."

ROBB FELDER

BEYOND THE GOLD

Jerry and Bob stood by Bob's truck and the sheriff by his SUV as the bulldozer was leveling the last of the ruins.

Finally, Jerry said, "I can't watch anymore. We better get going now. We've got to find the kids."

"Yes," Bob said, "And hopefully alive."

The snow was coming down pretty heavily now, with several inches already on the ground. The sheriff said, "I better get going too. I've got a ton of paperwork to do. Thankfully, we can finally close out the cold case of the murder of Lewis Feiffer. You guys let me know if you need help finding the kids, I can send out a couple deputies, or even get together a search party. You might start with that old barn on the hill across the highway and railroad. I saw that old Chevy truck parked there when I came by earlier. You guys drive carefully, this snow is going to make driving pretty tricky again."

"Thanks," Jerry said, "we'll keep you

posted. And could you let me know if you find Billy with my truck? Who knows where he was headed."

The sheriff left first and almost got stuck in the long driveway.

Bob said to his dad, worriedly, "We better get going as well. The bulldozer people have packed up and pulled out. We'll stop at that old barn across the way, on our way out. But if the kids aren't there, who knows where Frank took them and I don't know how much more searching we can do tonight. It's become black dark, and with this snowstorm, I don't think we can get around too much anymore tonight. I sure do hope the kids are somewhere inside."

They pulled out and made a stop at the old barn on the hill across the highway. Billy's old rusty brown Chevy truck was there, but there was no sign of the kids in the old barn and no sign that they had ever been there. The snow was now about six inches deep and coming down heavier than ever. The wind was beginning to blow the snow around. It was becoming a real blizzard.

"We might as well head back to town," Bob said. "We can call the sheriff and see what he recommends, but I don't think there's much anyone can do in this blizzard."

"I just hope the kids are somewhere safe, out of this storm. Hopefully still alive," Jerry said, "My guess is that Frank took them and locked them up in that third floor granary room of theirs, or possibly in the old barn."

He wasn't even thinking of the brewing chamber under the old slop kitchen, because, in his mind they had sealed it up completely when they broke out of it last spring.

* * * *

Ellen grabbed the lantern as they all scrambled over the rock pile and into the tunnel and climbed the rubble pile up to the opening in the tunnel ceiling. Brittany was the first one out. Ellen handed the lantern up to her, which was almost blown out by the howling wind of the blizzard outside. Ellen crawled out next, followed by Luke and Ryan. They all just stood there, confused at first. It was a very different world outside now, with the howling wind and driving snow. They realized they would have to get inside somewhere quickly. They knew they didn't want to go into the granary. That was Billy and Frank's lair, they had heard.

Finally Ryan shouted, over the wind, "I think I remember the barn being over this way," as he got the lantern from Brittany and led the way with the lantern flickering in the wind. He was right. Around a corner and about fifty yards ahead, they made their way to the barn. They worked their way around to a door and went in out of the howling blizzard.

"Maybe we can find some old hay to sleep

on," Ellen said.

"Probably in the loft," Ryan said, as he led the way down an alleyway alongside the cow mangers and found a ladder up to the old hay loft.

He climbed the ladder and found an old lantern hook next to the ladder and hung he lantern on it. They all climbed up and to their delight they found fresh hay. Apparently some farmer had rented out the old barn to store his new hay in. They each broke open a bale of the hay and made a nice soft warm bed of hay. Ryan went over and turned out the lantern and they all crawled into their cozy warm bed of hay, while outside, the first blizzard of winter raged on.

They were awakened again about two A.M. by voices outside. They heard voices, muffled by the hay and howling wind of the blizzard. It sounded like someone shouting orders to someone.

"Over here Hans, bring the team of horses around the wagon so we can get them hitched up," It was Joe shouting orders, "We've got to get the wagon loaded with another load of the half-barrels. We've got to get the load over to the feed mill warehouse in town. Tomorrow night the runners will pick up their loads to distribute to the speakeasy's in Detroit Lakes and Moorhead."

"What was that?" Brittany said as she was awakened by the voices.

"I heard it too," Luke said as he was also awakened.

"Probably just the wind," Ryan said, "Let's get back to sleep.

MYSTERY ON THE OTTER TAIL

* * * *

Bob headed the truck back towards Otter Falls. It was slow going. The road was very slippery with packed snow and ice. The snowplow had made one pass already, but the heavy snow and howling wind were just drifting the snow right back into the highway. As they approached the sharp curve in the highway, just before coming onto Otter Falls, they saw, up ahead, flashing lights right at the curve. Bob slowed way down for the curve and the flashing lights. As they approached, they noticed the sheriffs SUV with its flashing lights on the side of the curve. Bob crept past, and they saw a tow truck pulling a vehicle up the embankment.

"Looks like someone didn't make the curve," Bob said.

"Yah, it looks like that truck went over the edge and overturned and hit a tree. Boy, oh boy, I sure hope nobody got killed down there. Wait a darn minute, - - - -.that's my truck. Stop, Bob, stop, stop."

Bob pulled over, ahead of the tow truck and stopped. Jerry got out into the driving snow and howling wind and walked back to the sheriff's SUV.

The sheriff met him half way and said, "I was just about to call you. Yeah, that was Billy driving. Let's get into my SUV, out of the wind and I'll tell you what I know. The ambulance just left with Billy."

They got into the sheriff's SUV.

"On my way back into town, I was coming around this curve and luckily, just happened to see the taillights of your truck, down the embankment, overturned. Looks like Billy didn't make the curve and skidded over the edge, down the embankment and rolled the truck and skidded into a tree. I called it in right away, and got an ambulance out here. Meanwhile, I went down to check on him. He is in pretty rough shape. He was unconscious when I found him. He had been thrown from the truck when it rolled. He wasn't wearing a seat belt, of course. I'm not sure he'll make it, although he is one tough SOB. We'll get your truck into the Ford dealer in town. Looks like it will be a 'total'. I sure hope your kids are somewhere inside, out of this blizzard. Again, let me know if you need help in the morning, finding them."

"Thanks, for everything," Jerry said. "I just want to find the kids."

"Well, don't go out anymore tonight. Just hold up in your motel until morning and wait for the snowplows to clear the roads. They're predicting over a foot of snow.

* * * *

MYSTERY ON THE OTTER TAIL

The morning after, dawned with a bright new day. A blazing yellow sun was cutting its way up into a sea of bright blue. The blizzard was over. The four hay-mow sleepers awoke to the sound of a truck outside, struggling through the foot deep snow. Then, voices, muffled by all the hay inside and the deep snow outside. They held their breath in fear of who it might be down below. They had no need to fear any longer, but they were unaware that the man they deathly feared had met death himself the night before. They had still been trapped in the basement brew chamber when their feared nemesis, had met his own demise and was buried forever under hundreds of tons of debris in the cellar of the ancient brewery ruins. They waited in frozen silence as the voices, muffled by all the fresh snow, suddenly stopped.

Jerry and Bob had gone into the old granary, and up to the infamous third floor, but of course, the kids weren't there. Then more voices as Jerry and Bob came out.

"I didn't really think they would be there," Jerry said, "But I bet I know where they are."

He led Bob down and around back to the ruins of the ancient slop kitchen chimney. There, sure enough, was the hole, down into the tunnel and the brew room. They climbed down in and yelled for the kids, but of course, no answer. They came back up and started back to the truck, thinking that they should call the sheriff for help.

Suddenly Bob said, "Wait; how about the old

barn?"

They opened the barn door and Bob yelled all the kids names; Ellen, - - - Brittany. - - - Ryan, - - -, Luke. In the loft, hay went flying as they all four leaped out of their hay beds.

Ellen yelled, "Dad, is that you?"

"Yes, it's us," Came back the reply.

"Were up here in the loft," they all yelled together, "we'll be right down, as they raced down the ladder, one by one, their hair and clothes covered with bits and pieces of the alfalfa hay. It was a joyous reunion next to the old cow manger.

"Oh, my God, the nightmare is over," Ellen said as she hugged her dad, and Brittany hugged her grandpa Jerry. Then, a group hug.

They all left the barn and headed for Bob's truck.

"Wait, what's this, Dad?" Bob said as he led them over to the tracks in the snow.

"It looks like some kind of wagon tracks," Jerry replied, "And look there's hoof prints in the snow, like from a team of horses."

They followed the tracks around the side of the barn and down onto the old road that used to go into Otter Falls. But as they looked at the tracks they seemed to fade away into the distance.

"Ok, let's get out of this place," Ryan said.

"This place is just way too creepy," Ellen said, "I swear it's haunted everywhere you go."

"Let's get something to eat," Luke said, "We're starving."

They all crammed into Bob's truck and

MYSTERY ON THE OTTER TAIL

headed into town. On the way, Jerry explained what had happened to his truck.

"I'll have to check with the Otter Falls Ford dealer and see about getting my truck fixed or replaced."

They headed to the Lakes Cafe for breakfast.

Ellen said, "You'll have to catch us up on what happened after we were kidnapped."

Jerry called the sheriff's office to report that the kids had been found, safe and unharmed. They all wolfed down a huge breakfast, since none of them had eaten since yesterday's breakfast. After breakfast, Luke, Ryan, Brittany and Ellen all wanted to know what happened in the brew house basement after they were kidnapped by Frank.

Jerry and Bob took turns, explaining what happened with the confrontation with Billy and Frank and the sheriff, and with Billy's escape with Jerry's truck. And Franks wrong turn in the cellars, and the concussion from his gun collapsing the floor above on top of him and burying him forever, under hundreds of tons of rubble while clinging to the gold ingot.

"Good riddance," Ellen said, "That man was nothing but a monster. But Billy, on the other hand, didn't seem to be as twisted as Frank. At least he didn't want to kill and rape everybody."

"But that means that all of the rest of the gold is also buried under tons and tons of rubble." Brittany said.

"Yah, I'm afraid so," Jerry said, "It looks like

instead of gold, we have silver. Thousands of silver dollars. It'll just take us some time to convert it into spendable money."

DEER HUNTING AT LAST

"Speaking of time," Ryan said, "I just remembered, tomorrow is the opening of deer hunting season and uncles, Andy and Adam will be arriving soon to join us. Does everyone still want to go?"

"Well, sure," Bob said, "We may as well. The girls and I already have our deer stands set up."

"Ryan and I will need to get ours set up yet today," Luke said. "We'll also have to find a spot for Andy and Adam to set up their stands."

"Ok," Bob said, "I'll give you guys a ride out to the river later. This morning, I need to get Grandpa over to the Ford dealer to check on his truck."

Jerry paid he tab and they all left for their motel. The girls decided to stay put in their room for the day. They needed to shower and get cleaned up and recover from the shock of yesterday, and get their gear ready for tomorrow's hunt. The guys all left in a little while, after showering and changing. Bob dropped Jerry off at the Ford dealer and he and Luke and Ryan went out to the river to set up their tree stands in the woods, just north of the big spring.

Andy and Adam arrived a short time later and the guys all left in a little while. Jerry, Andy and Adam discussed their options for a place to set up their stands. "There's a large hill on the east side of the Ottertail river, just opposite the big spring," Jerry said, "You can get to it by crossing at the bridge and walking the river's edge up about a quarter mile."

As they struggled walking into the woods in the foot deep snow, they noticed the total absence of any deer signs.

"How will we ever be able to find those deer runs?" Ryan said, "And any other deer signs."

"It will be a challenging hunt tomorrow." Bob said, "During a big snowfall, the deer typically will bed down and stay put, sometimes for a day or two. There is no way to know if tomorrow they will be up, going back and forth to their feeding grounds. The good news is that if and when they will get up to feed, with the snow covering the ground and the low-growing brush, they will be a lot easier to see, albeit almost impossible to hear. Thus is the challenge of the hunt.

After a couple of hours of struggling through the foot deep snow trying to find the deer runs, they had their stands up. They headed back to town and found that Jerry had just completed the paperwork to get his 'totaled' truck replaced with a new one. Jerry stopped at the motel and picked up

MYSTERY ON THE OTTER TAIL

the girls and they all met at McDonalds for lunch. After lunch, Jerry said he was going over to the hospital to see if Billy had survived the crash.

"What does it matter," Ellen said, "He was a bad dude too, maybe not as bad as Frank was, but bad enough."

"Well, I've got this feeling about him. Maybe, if he does survive, he might have a change of heart; without Frank, and without the gold to torment his mind."

Jerry went over to the hospital. The rest of the group went back to the motel to relax after the last couple of harrowing days. He got to the hospital and checked in at the information desk and said he was an acquaintance of Billy Buchanen, They directed him to the Intensive Care Unit. Billy had undergone surgery to remove the bullet from the sheriff's gun, and repair several ribs and other broken bones from the crash. Jerry was allowed only a few minutes with Billy, who had been out of surgery for only a few hours , and was just regaining consciousness, He couldn't talk because he had a tube down his throat, and IV lines and tubes and monitors everywhere. The nurse gave Billy a pad and pen. On it he wrote just two words; 'Blood-Brother --'.

Jerry took the note as Billy fell back to sleep. He had no idea what the note meant. He just stood there for a minute holding on to it.

"Maybe," he thought, "Billy had a brother that he wanted Jerry to call and talk too."

But he had no idea where Billy's brother might be, or how to get ahold of him. Finally, he left, very confused. He knew, he would have to come back in a few days to find out about this mysterious brother.

* * * *

Dawn was still almost three hours away. Four thirty was an un-Godly hour to be getting up. Yet, all across Minnesota, alarm clocks were going off. Coffee pots were being turned on, as about one hundred thousand, red-eyed, groggy humans were struggling to come back to life. Like a huge army of zombies, ready to take up arms against an enemy of completely innocent and meek members of the animal kingdom. This was truly the dawn of the slaughter of the innocents. It was a scenario that had been playing out since the dawning of the human race. Meat had to be procured for the upcoming winter. Survival was at stake.

At the Otter Motel in Otter Falls, alarm clocks were being slapped down, until a glimmer of consciousness forced them to make a choice; sleep, or meat? Sleep or, a chance at that ten point buck that was coming slowly to the forefront now, of the decision making process. For all involved in this ritual, the ten point buck wins out. The army rises up and prepares for battle.

"Ohhh," Ellen moaned, "I'm just not sure I want to do this. It's way too early."

MYSTERY ON THE OTTER TAIL

"Oh, come on Ellen," Brittany coached, "you know you'll have fun once we get going."

With that, they slowly arose and completed the bathroom ritual. Teeth were brushed, faces washed, hair brushed, but makeup not applied. Nor anything smelly they - -were instructed. The deer had one of the keenest senses of smell of all mammals, they were told. Pretty much the same morning ritual in the boy's rooms. Soon the troops were all similarly uniformed and headed downstairs for breakfast. A 'hunters special' served at five A.M., eaten in silence by the half-awakened army of the blaze orange. There were simply no experiences yet to be shared. Back upstairs to dawn heavy coats and caps of blaze orange, and of course the necessary armament and ammo.

The drive out to the farm on the river, more silence. The silence would prevail until shots rang and meat was slaughtered. Jerry and Bob struggled with their trucks through the foot deep snow, which had stiffened up overnight, where it had drifted. They came in with lights off, and parked behind the hog barn ruins, in what had once been one of the outside pens, although the fences no longer existed. They very quietly exited the trucks, being careful not to slam doors. They grabbed their guns from the back and carefully began to find the trail that would take them up-river, to the hunting grounds. The same process was executed at the river bridge where the two brothers; Andy and Adam made their way to the hill-top across from the big spring. At this hour, it was still very black out. Sunrise was still two hours away. It was partly cloudy with a three quarter moon passing in and out of the black clouds. There was not yet that sliver of light at the eastern horizon signaling the coming dawn. The night time critters that they were pursuing were still grazed in silence in the open spaces of the prairie. Only with daylight would they disappear into the shadows.

The troops moved carefully and silently down the trail they had made in the snow yesterday that would lead them to their tree stands. They dared not look over their shoulder, to the right, where the ghostly old barn and granary stood in the blackness. They dared not be reminded of the nightmares that had occurred there. The pain and anguish of their, 'near-death' experience was still too raw in their consciousness.

They arrived at their tree stands and found the cords they had suspended from their seats. They were reminded of the safety rules told them by Jerry. Never climb a tree stand with a loaded gun. Pull your unloaded gun up by a cord, when you are safely in your seat. Keep the safety belt around you at all times. Now, the waiting began. It was about six twenty, and the legal shooting time was five minutes past seven. Slowly, ever so slowly, the faintest streak of light appeared on the eastern horizon between the clouds, as the eastern sky slowly faded from black to a pale blue-gray with streaks of red-orange. This was soon followed by the glimpse of actual sunlight at 7:05. However, this was the time when the temperature dropped to the lowest point of the night. This morning it was predicted to drop to nine or ten degrees above zero. After sitting still for so long, the fingers and toes began to feel numb, yet tingly and painful, all at the same time. This was prevented by chemical 'hot' packs stuffed into mittens and boots.

    Jerry didn't join the troop into the tree stands. He had to choose instead, a stand on the ground. Two artificial hip joints prevented him from climbing ladders. But, he didn't mind. He was a bit, 'old-school', and preferred a spot on the ground. He found one of the old oak trees that had been blown down by the wind, out on that point overlooking the tamarack swamp. He situated himself comfortably on it. He had a hard time focusing on hunting, however. He just had too much on his mind with everything that had transpired over the last couple of days. He was having guilt feelings about not being able to get the last of the gold out for the kids and grandkids. And there was that new mystery with Billy's brother. Who was he, and where was he? Was Frank actually Billy's brother? Billy wouldn't know about what happened to Frank yet, because he had taken off before it happened. As the sun came up, he was still puzzling over it. And worse, as the morning light started to appear, he could see through the tamaracks, the outline of the remnants of the old farm, but where the brewery once proudly stood; nothing - - -. Gone forever - - -. He knew he would have to get over it, but there was so much history there, so very much family history.

Just about sunrise, he heard some noise down below at the edge of the tamaracks. He looked carefully and saw just a pair of does, pawing into the snow, getting something to eat. But, no buck yet.

Ellen sat frozen, in more ways than just from the cold. Just as the sun broke into the horizon, at 7:05, she heard the faintest sound, sort of a faint swooshing sound, like a whisper, off to her left. Then they appeared;- - - three does, moseying down the shallow wash, heading for their bedding area. She held her breath as she carefully and quietly took her gun off of safety. She waited patiently as they passed beneath her. She knew she couldn't shoot does, only bucks. She waited patiently some more as the does disappeared down the wash, then, sure enough, just as her dad and grandpa Jerry had taught her, about fifty yards behind the does, there was a buck following. Ellen waited, just to make sure. The buck had a very nice rack. It looked to be about six points. She slowly raised her rifle and peered through the scope. He was still too far out, and didn't present a good angle. She waited and watched him some more through her scope waiting for a good angle, but as she was following him down the wash toward her and presented a good angle for a shot, the buckle on her gun strap clinked against a steel bar on her deer stand, just as she fired. The buck bolted, up the far side of the wash, and disappeared behind some bushes, but reappeared further down the wash out of range, trotting after the does again.

Brittany was just about dozing in her stand, down at the base of the wash, when the shot jarred her back into alertness. She quickly took her gun off of safety as the three does came trotting down the wash, heading for cover in the swamp. She too, waited patiently for them to pass beneath her. When they did, she looked back up the wash, expecting to see a buck following the three does. After several minutes not seeing one, she assumed that the shot she heard from Ellen's gun had brought him down. Now with the three does disappearing into the heavy brush of the swamp, she was preparing to get down from her stand to go help Ellen. But, just as she clicked the safety back on, and was about to eject the shells, she heard a somewhat soft rustling sound, across and up the wash. She quickly clicked her safety off again, and slowly and quietly raised her gun and aimed it in the direction of the sound, and peered into the scope. There, on the far side of the wash, coming out into the open and slowly moseying down towards the does in the swamp, was a real nice sized, four-point buck. She put the crosshairs on him as he took one more step and exposed a beautiful broadside shot. Brittany slowly squeezed the trigger. The report sound resonated up and down the wash, and Brittany watched as the young buck went down and tumbled halfway down the side of the wash, but was struggling to get up again. She still had the crosshairs on him and had a perfect front quarter shot. She fired again and the buck went down again, for good. The shot exploded into his heart and severed his arteries.

Brittany, brought the rifle down and unloaded, and tied it to the cord and lowered it to the ground. She climbed down after it. Up the wash, Ellen was doing the same thing. Brittany picked up her rifle and began walking towards her kill, about thirty yards away.

Ellen met her there and said, "What do we do now?"

"Well, my dad, Adam, explained how to gut a deer, but I've never actually seen it done before."

"Me neither. Wait, that's not my deer. Mine had six points."

Just then Bob came walking over from his stand further up the river.

"I heard three shots. What's the story here?"

"Well," Ellen started to explain, "I shot first. I got off a shot at a nice six-pointer, but my strap buckle hit on my stand and spooked him, so I missed him. When I heard Brittany shoot, I assumed that was my deer, which I had missed."

"When I shot my deer," Brittany said, "I just assumed that it was the deer that Ellen had missed, only, mine is a four-pointer, and Ellen's was a six."

"So, that means that my six-pointer is still out

there," Ellen said.

"Yes it is," Bob said, "and I saw him. Just after you fired your shot, Ellen, I heard a noise in the brush along the river, and then coming up along the fence line at the edge of the farm. I had my back to the fence line, facing the washout, but, I turned, and saw this nice six-pointer. Only I couldn't shoot, because just over the fence line is the neighbor's house and barnyard.

"So, he's gone now, out of our area?" Ellen asked.

"No, I doubt it," Bob said, there's nothing out beyond that fence line for cover, it's just open prairie fields. I'm sure he'll be back here in the woods for cover. Well, let's get this one gutted and back to town for processing." Well, let's get this one gutted and back to town for processing." Just then, they all heard several shots being fired; coming from across the river.

"That's coming from Adam and Andy's area," Brittany said, "I hope they got something too."

"I hope it's not my six-pointer," Ellen said.

Bob proceeded to show the girls how to gut a deer, and put a tag on it. After that was accomplished, they all took turns dragging the deer up the wash and out along the edge of the prairie towards where the trucks were parked. On the way back, as they passed the wash where Ryan and Luke were stationed, the boys got down out of their stands and came up the wash to see Brittany's nice four-pointer.

Bob said to them; after the girls had told their story, "You guys stay put. That nice six-pointer will be back in the area before too long. He's got those three does down in the swamp that he wants. They continued on to the trucks, and Jerry met them.

After hearing their story, he said to Bob, "Why don't I take the girls and the deer into town? I have some more insurance forms to sign at the Ford dealer. That way, you can go back and maybe get a shot at that six-pointer."

They loaded Brittany's deer into Jerry's truck, and Jerry, Ellen and Brittany headed into town. They dropped the deer off at the Otter Falls Processing Plant. Brittany ordered lots of venison jerky and sausage, and some steaks and chops. They said it would be ready in about two weeks.

Just as Brittany was ordering her venison meat cuts, Andy and Adam came in with also a nice four pointer.

"We got him on the east side of that small hill," Adam said, "He was trying to cut across that hill heading west, probably to cross the river and hook up with those does that you guys had seen."

"Wait, wait," Jerry said, "What do you mean; 'we'?"

"Well, it's like this," Andy started to explain, "We were sitting in our double stand, and saw this four-pointer, just at the crest of the hill, running down towards us. I fired first, but missed. The buck, instead of running away, kept coming towards us."

"Then I fired and missed, because the buck was running full speed at a really bad angle," Adam said, "So, then we both fired at the same time. The deer went down, but when we got over to it, only one shot had actually hit the deer."

"So one of us hit the deer," Andy said, "and one of us missed. We'll never know who's shot brought him down."

After 'they' ordered 'their' venison cuts, Andy said, "Well I think Adam and I will head out and get back home yet tonight. We've got enough venison, what with Brittany's and 'our' four pointers. Thanks for showing us that hill across the river, Dad. I think we'll be back again next year."

Jerry took Ellen and Brittany back to the motel so they could shower and get changed. Jerry waited in the lobby. When the girls came down, they said they wanted to go downtown and do some shopping. Jerry dropped them off and went to the Ford dealer to conclude his insurance paperwork. After that, he went back to the motel and took a nice long nap, while he waited for the girls to call for a ride. They woke him at about five P.M. and said they would meet up at the 'Ales and Eats' restaurant for dinner. Shortly after they met, Bob, Luke and Ryan joined them.

"How'd it go, this afternoon?" Jerry asked.

"Well, we didn't see much of anything," Bob

replied,

"I think that buck from this morning, stayed well hidden, down in the swamp after being shot at this morning," Ryan said.

"We saw some more does," Luke reported, "but no buck."

After dinner they discussed the deer situation some more, and then agreed they should all go back out to the farm again, in the morning, and try for that six pointer.

Jerry cautioned them to not pass up a chance at a smaller buck, if they saw one. He said that there was no guarantee that the six-pointer would show up at all tomorrow.

He told them about his visit to see Billy at the hospital, and the mysterious note that Billy wrote about his brother. He called over to the hospital to see how Billy was doing. They said, better, but still critical. They had removed his tube, and said maybe tomorrow he would be able to talk. They all went back to their motel, watched a little TV, and crashed into bed. It had been a long day, and four thirty, A.M. comes very early.

The next morning at four thirty, it was the same routine; bathroom, breakfast, out to the deer stands and wait for sunrise. It was another very cold morning, in the single digits for the temperature. But it was very cloudy, like it could snow again. Hopefully, they could get that big buck before the deer bedded down for another snow storm.

Just after sunrise, they all heard a shot. It was

that big buck. They all just knew it.

The three does, the same three, came down the wash again, after feeding in the hay field all night. The big six pointer was following again. Today, he was a lot more cautious and followed from the top edge of the wash where he could see better and catch any human scents. Today, however, it was a different wash, and it was Ryan who first watched the does pass almost right under his stand. He looked back up the wash. He saw nothing at first. But then, just as he was beginning to become disappointed, he spotted, just a quick glimpse of movement, over on the other edge of the wash. His pulse quickened to about a hundred and twenty beats a minutes as he quietly switched off the gun safety and slowly, ever so slowly raised his rifle until the crosshairs were right on the chest of the six pointer, and slowly pulled the trigger. The sound of the shot resonated up and down the river valley.

The other hunters all came down out of their trees and began disassembling their stands. The hunt was over. They had gotten the two bucks that they wanted. Jerry told them, that was all the meat they needed. No sense getting piggish about it. He said that he had seen another buck, down in the tamaracks, but they should leave it, to breed the does, and replenish the herd for next year.

They got back into town well before noon. Jerry took Ryan and his nice six-pointer to the processing plant. Ryan got to decide which venison cuts he wanted. He ordered venison jerky, venison sausage, and some venison cheesy brats, that he knew his grandpa would like. The rest of the meat he ordered into steaks, chops and roasts, which he knew his mom, Brenda would make into some wonderful venison meals.

Back at the motel, everyone packed up their gear and clothes and got ready to check out. They carried down the three very heavy beer cases full of the ancient silver dollar coins and loaded them into the trucks. There was some urgency with their packing up and leaving. There was a prediction out for another foot of snow. They all met in the motel restaurant for one last meal together before heading home. After their lunch, they briefly discussed all the events of the last week.

"Wow," Ellen said, "What started out as a deer hunting trip, sure turned out to be a whole lot more."

"Yeah," Luke agreed, "It was like a deer hunting, slash, treasure hunting trip."

"I think it was more like a trip of many phases," Brittany said, "There was, set up deer stand phase, treasure hunt phase, more treasure hunt, slash terror, nightmare, kidnapped phase, rescue phase, and finally, the actual deer hunt phase."

"Well," Ryan said. "Over all, it was a really exciting time, in spite of that one terrorizing night in that haunted dungeon. We did find some treasure, and we had a very successful deer hunt."

Well, no gold," Bob said, "But we found a lot

of those silver dollars to go through, and convert into cash. Maybe some of them will be quite rare and valuable."

"There's still a lot of that gold buried under the old brewery ruins," Jerry said. "Maybe some future generation will decide to try and find it, and dig it up and become very rich, with the price of gold continuously going up. Now, before everyone takes-off, there's one favor I would ask you to do. I would like you to come with me, over to the hospital to see and talk to Billy Buchanen. I need to talk to him and find out about this brother of his."

ROBB FELDER

THE REVELATION

There were some protests about seeing this man who had terrorized them over the past week. But in the end, they all came with Jerry to the hospital. They arrived at the hospital to find that Billy had been moved out of intensive care, and could have visitors, only for a limited time. The group slowly and reluctantly entered his room. Jerry approached the bed. Billy looked ghostly pale and in a lot of pain from the gunshot wound and broken bones from the truck accident. A far cry from the vibrant, angry man who had terrorized them all for the past week, and Jerry for the last six months.

"I got your note from the other day," Jerry said.

"Note?" Billy said, hoarsely. almost in a whisper. Apparently he didn't remember writing a note.

'Blood-Brother," he said, hoarsely, a little louder this time.

"Yes, your brother, I came to talk about your brother. Was Frank your brother?"

"No, Jerry, YOU are my blood-brother," he almost shouted this time.

"No, no, you must be confused, maybe from

all the painkillers. Who is this brother of yours?"

"You, dammit, Jerry, you're my blood-brother. don'cha under stand? Let me explain."

"This is just crazy," Jerry said to the group, as they gathered closer, with their mouths hanging open, waiting for Billy to explain.

"Here is the story that my mother Morning Dove told to me. She had been in love with your father, Joe when he left to fight in World War 1. While he was away at war, her dad Thunder Cloud, got into a big fight with his brother, New Moon. They fought about their kids marrying white men. Finally my Grandpa packed up Mom and took her with him up into Canada. They stayed there for almost ten years. Finally, Mom couldn't stand him constantly pushing her to marry an Indian, so she left Canada and returned to the camp at Otter Falls. My grandfather, Thunder Cloud followed her several years later. My mom and your dad began seeing each other again. They dated for several years, and began talking marriage again. However in about 1933, your grandfather, August wanted your dad to take that job at the brewery in Alexandria. My mom and your dad had some heated discussions about it. Your dad finally left, of course, and they broke up in 1935."

Billy paused and took a sip of water for his parched throat. Then he continued.

"A short time later, my mom realized she was pregnant with me. She had disgraced the family, first because she got pregnant by a white man, and secondly, because there was no way that she was going to get married. Back then, that was a really bad thing. So Grandpa Thunder Cloud threw her out. Mom moved into Otter Falls where I was born. My mom struggled to make ends meet. She couldn't get child support from your dad, and in fact, she never told him about me. She didn't dare approach August or the family either. That just wasn't done back then. Nor was there any welfare assistance back then, for an Indian with a child. She worked two jobs to support us and send me to school. I got as far as the eighth grade, then, I had to drop out and help support us. Shortly after I left school, Mom met a real nice guy named Fred Buchanen. I really liked Fred. When they got married, he adopted me and I got his last name."

"So, why did you hate us Feiffer's so bad? It seemed like you were always cussing us out."

"When your dad and mom moved back to the brewery and farm, I just started developing these hostile feelings for your Feiffer family. You Feiffer's had it all, a great family, and a great life. That's why we were never friends in school, although we were in the same grade. I really, really hated you guys. Because I knew I was your brother."

"So how did you find out about all the gold in the brewery, and farm?"

"When me and Frank got fired from our jobs up in Fargo, Fred got us the jobs as security for the cheese company, because he knew about the gold and wanted us to help him look for it. As he got real old, he thought he could get us to find it for him. Back in Prohibition, Fred worked for your uncle Lewis as a bootleg runner. Fred got busted along with your uncle, and was in prison with him. That's when Lewis told my stepdad about the gold. My mom and stepdad both died back in the seventies, but we couldn't start looking for the gold until the cheese company closed, because we weren't allowed to go into the brewery, except to throw the vagrants out."

"What about Lewis?" Bob asked.

"Lewis never told Fred exactly where the gold was hidden, because he really didn't know. That's why he couldn't tell Frank, and Frank killed him. That damn Frank always want'in to kill somebody. Did he escape from the brewery that night or did he get arrested?'

Neither," Jerry explained, "He was killed when an upper floor collapsed on him. He's lying buried under tons and tons of debris down in the basement of the brewery."

"Ohhh, that's so sad," Billy said with tears in his eyes. Frank was my good buddy for all those years, since we served in Vietnam together. But he was badly damaged and deranged from the war. He never got the help he needed, to recover. The VA did a lousy job back then, of rehabbing psychologically damaged soldiers."

"I believe that's called PTSD," Jerry said

"That's some story Billy," Bob said, "how do we know if we should believe you?"

"Well," Billy said, "We could have one of

them DNA tests done."

Just then a nurse came in and told them that their time was up. They all trooped out, shaking their heads and mumbling among themselves.

"I just can't believe all that," Ellen said, "That would mean Billy is our great uncle."

"I know," Ryan said, "That's going to take a long time to get used to."

"Can you imagine how Grandpa feels?" Brittany said, "He now has a brother that he never knew he had."

"He must really be in total shock," Luke said.

Suddenly, after hearing Billy's story and Billy calling Jerry his 'blood-brother', something clicked in Jerry's mind. It all came back to him in a rush. The vision that he had at the Springs when he first returned to Otter Falls that he had dismissed as a crazy dream, and all the crazy events of the past summer were suddenly all making sense. He now knew what he had to do.

Jerry stayed behind for a minute and said to Billy, "Billy, if all that is really true, I should start caring for you like a real brother would. They have a very good in-house rehab program right here in the hospital. Could I sign you up for it?"

"Yes, brother, I really would like to turn my life around."

THE END

ROBB FELDER

EPILOGUE

Snow; it seems never ending, once it starts. The icy northwest wind was picking up the top layer of the latest snowfall and whisking it across highway ten, north of St. Cloud, in the open prairie country of northwestern Minnesota. It created a flowing sea of white at a diagonal across the roadway. While one could not truly call it a 'white-out' because it was not totally blinding. It did, however totally obscure the entire roadway, erasing the lane markings and the white center line. Out on this sea of white, a new red Ford pickup truck navigated its way northwesterly, heading for Otter Falls. It was early December, the temperature was well below zero, and the sun was low in the pale blue sky.

Inside the truck, Barbara was saying to Jerry, "I'm so glad the hospital finally resolved their staffing issues so I could come with on this trip. After all your trips back to Otter Falls, I'm finally getting to come with."

"Yah," Jerry replied, "It's so nice to be on a road trip again with you. We haven't been away together for about a year. I'm so glad that I've finally cleared up some of the mysteries of the old Feiffer family farm and brewery."

"Yeah, and we've become quite rich from all that bootleg gold and money you found."

"Well we've now got enough to send our grandkids through college. But, now it's time to disperse it to all of my Feiffer siblings. It's a part of all of our heritages."

"We still don't have all the gold and silver converted into cash yet. But I agree with you, we shouldn't have to do all the work. So we're just going to divide up the rest of it, as is. Everyone could use the money this time of year."

"Yah, we'll start with the most needy ones first. That would be our new-found brother."

"I'm so glad for you, that the DNA test proved that Billy is in fact your half-brother." refill. Jerry had to rest his eyes from struggling through the shifting drifting landscape, constantly trying to determine where the highway lanes should be. In another hour, they turned off the four-lane and drove past where the historic Otter Falls Brewery once stood. Now, there was nothing remaining of the once proud and beautiful brewery building except a flat, plot of snow-covered land, on the hillside alongside the Ottertail River, on the north-side of the railroad tracks. It was as if a very large piece of the history of the Otter Falls area

MYSTERY ON THE OTTER TAIL

had been erased, gone forever, the product of corporate greed, paranoia, and ignorance. Jerry pulled over and stopped in front of the place. They both just sat there in silence for several minutes.

Finally Barbara spoke, "It's hard to believe what you said, that there is another couple of million dollars worth of gold buried somewhere under all the rubble. I can't even imagine what it must feel like for you, having your family history erased in such a manner, after all that's happened there over the years, and especially over the last six months."

"I'll tell you that it makes one feel so very helpless against the gigantic corporate entities of our world today. It just pains me to even drive by the place, which is why I haven't come back here for forty years, and probably won't again for another forty years. But, for now, we have some business to attend to."

They arrived in Otter Falls, and first went to the bank. Jerry rented another safe-deposit box. He went downstairs and opened his first safe-deposit box. He withdrew one of the gold bars and put it into the new safe-deposit box, and went back upstairs and withdrew ten thousand dollars from the account he had opened last spring and put it into a small folio bag. The next stop was the Otter

Falls Hospital. They signed in at the Rehab department and asked to see Billy Buchanen. They were led to a small lounge area, where they waited for about ten minutes. Finally, Billy entered, looking much improved from the last time Jerry had seen him. He had shaved and gotten a haircut. He had on new clothes, and had obviously bathed.

"Wow!" Jerry said, "You look like a whole different person."

"Yeah, brother, they got me all primed and, shined up. I feel like I'm a new person."

"Well, Billy, I'd like you to meet my wife, Barbara."

"Pleased ta meet ya ma'am," Billy responded.

"Well. I'm pleased to meet you too. I've heard so much about you. I'm glad you seem to be recovering nicely from that bad accident."

"Yah, hopefully I'm recovering in more ways than one. They got a really good program here. First, let me apologize for being such a bad-ass. Ya know, I just got so wrapped up in that whole gold thing. I never would have shot ya though, ya know. I got so much guilt to work through now, for both you and for Frank. My good buddy Frank, we was such good buddies all those years. We met in the Army. But, the war just destroyed his mind. He was never able to get the help he needed from the VA. Neither was I, although, now the VA has agreed to pay for my rehab here. I think I've come a long way since I've been in the program. I think I'm ready for the next level. At this point I would really like to get back together with my wife, Ruth Ann, if she'll have me back."

"Well, maybe we could talk to her," Barbara said, "and see how she would feel about reconciling with you."

"Ya, that 'recon' word," Billy said, "that's what we need."

"Okay, then," Jerry said, "That sounds like a good plan. We'll go talk to her tomorrow, and let you know how she feels about it."

So, Jerry and Barbara left the Rehab Center and went over to the Otter Falls Motel and checked in for the night. They had dinner at the Ales and Eats Restaurant, then returned to their motel room and googled the name Ruth Ann Buchanen to get her address and a phone number and called her to set up a meeting for the next day.

In the morning, they had a late breakfast at the motel, then left to find Billy's wife, Ruth Ann. She lived in an apartment building on the north side of Otter Falls with her daughter, Faith and

Billy's teen-age grandson, Joseph. Jerry rang the entry buzzer and she let them in. He introduced himself and Barbara.

"I'm pleased to finally meet you," Ruth Ann said, "Billy has told me so much about you over the years. But what brings you back to Otter Falls? Have you spoken to him recently?"

"Oh, very much so," Barbara joined in, "In the last six months they have spoken quite a bit. Go ahead, Jerry, you explain."

Jerry began to explain about the events of the last six months, about their quest for the bootlegger's gold, and Frank's death and Billy's accident with his truck. He told her about Billy's rehab and change of heart, and Billy's finally admitting that he was Jerry's half-brother.

"I really do believe that Billy has turned a corner in his life, and I think that with Frank out of his life and the quest for the gold over, he can really become a different person. He's worked really hard in rehab to face up to his alcoholism, and ways to deal with it. He has now expressed a real desire to reconcile his relationship with you."

"Wow!" Ruth Ann said, "This a little overwhelming. I think that I'll need some time to digest all this."

"I certainly don't blame you," Barbara said, Think it over and let us know if there's anything we can do. Take this one step at a time. Maybe just start by talking to each other."

Jerry and Barbara gave her their phone number and dropped her off at her home and said to call if they could help in any way. They decided to go downtown for lunch.

After lunch, Barbara said, "I've noticed, they have some cute little boutiques here in Otter Falls. Maybe we could do some Christmas shopping."

Later, they got a phone call from Ruth Ann.

"I've thought about it all day, and talked it over with my daughter, Faith, and grandson Joseph. We've all decided to give Billy another chance and at least talk to him. But I would like you guys to come with me for support. Would that be okay?"

"Yes, we'd be glad to," Jerry said, "We'll be over to pick you up in a few minutes."

The three of them arrived at the rehab center and signed in. This time, they were shown to a conference room, where one of the counselors met them. They all introduced themselves. The counselor said that Billy had made very good progress so far, but had a ways to go before he completed the program. Billy came in and took a seat. He thanked Jerry and Barbara for bringing Ruth Ann in.

"My God," Ruth Ann said, "I hardly recognized you. You're all cleaned up and shaved, and have a haircut and new clothes. It looks like you really are trying to turn your life around."

"Ya," Billy said, "I've really been working on it, and I want you back in my life again."

With that Jerry and Barbara got up to leave, saying they would wait in the waiting room. The counselor stayed, however. After the visit, they all said their good-byes. Jerry, Barbara and Ruth Ann found a nice restaurant and ordered dinner. While they waited for the food, Barbara asked Ruth Ann how she was feeling,

"Oh, I'm feeling so positive right now. This is the best I have felt in years, since before Billy got on that 'gold fever' of his. I really think we're going to make it this time. Now I'll have to find us a new place to live when he finishes rehab."

After dinner, Jerry gave the folio with the money in it to Ruth Ann along with the safe-deposit box key. "This should help you two get started again. Just a word of caution though, about the safe-deposit box. Don't open it or tell Billy about it until he completes his rehab. We wouldn't want him to take any shortcuts in his program."

MYSTERY ON THE OTTER TAIL

They dropped Ruth Ann off at her place as she thanked them again for everything. Jerry and Barbara checked out of their motel. Snow was starting to fall again as they headed for home, out across the white sea of drifting, flowing snow.

They followed the drifting snow southeasterly across the whitened prairie and across the now frozen Ottertail River, past the place where the Feiffer Pioneer family had once carved a living out of the wilderness, - - - now frozen in time. All of the history now buried forever beneath the drifting snows of Minnesota.

ROBB FELDER

ACKNOWLEDGEMENTS

I would first like to express my thanks to my beautiful wife Barbara for all the love and support, and the patience she has given me in this endeavor. She has been such a phenomenal help with the spelling and grammar, and the multiple proof readings.

Thanks to our daughter, Brenda, for the proof readings of the multiple versions and additions of the story.

Thanks to artist; Carla Fellerer for her design work on the covers.

Thanks to Marlene, Marcia, Laura, Brenda, Robert, David, Jenna & Travis, Brianna, Zachery, Colby, Ellen, Brittany, Adam, Andy, Ryan, Luke, Kira, McKenna, all of whom appear in the story, and all of the Fellerer's who have gone before us: Andrew and Anna, Joe and Alice, Frank, Lewis, Henry and Kate and Rose.

Thanks also to the History Museum of East Ottertail County in Perham, Minnesota, for their help with providing the background history of the Perham area.

A special thanks to Zachery and Colby; the great-great grandsons of August and Annie, for inspiring me to write these books and help build the diorama of the Feiffer farm and brewery, which resides in the East Ottertail County museum.

* * * * * * * * *

Go to WWW.otterfallspublishing.com to see more background about these new books in the series:
PIONEERS ON THE OTTERTAIL
MYSTERY ON THE OTTERTAIL
ADVENTURES ON THE OTTERTAIL
RETURN TO OTTER FALLS

Take a look at the new releases by;
ROBB FELDER

LAST FLIGHT OF THE SNOWBIRDS

THE COLD COLD WAR

AND;
DEATH OF A BREWERY
To be available late summer, 2019

ABOUT THE AUTHOR

ROBB FELDER Is a Vietnam Veteran. He attended the University of Alaska and the University of Minnesota. He grew up in the brewery and on the farm talked about in the story. This is his second novel in the Otter Falls Series. Robb is retired from a successful career as a computer applications software designer. He and his wife Barbara live in a suburb of the Twin Cities of Minnesota.

www.ingramcontent.com/pod-product-compliance
Lightning Source LLC
Chambersburg PA
CBHW070538010526
44118CB00012B/1166